Wedding Cakes
From Start to Finish

Elaine MacGregor

Souvenir Press

ACKNOWLEDGEMENTS

I would like to thank my husband, without whom this book would not be possible,
my children who are my most demanding critics,
Zul, my photographer, and Catherine, his assistant, Jan Cohen, who has done so much of the typing,
the rest of the staff at Woodnutt's for helping where they could and, last but not least,
my bank manager, without whom this book would not be necessary.

Thanks also to British Bakels for the Pettinice used for covering the sugarpaste cakes and the chocolate compound used for
coating Cake 8—Chocoholic's Dream, and to J. F. Renshaws for the marzipan used on all the cakes.

The glass church shown in the Winter Wedding cake was made by Mr Cliff Durant, of Glimmer Glass,
2A New Street, Brighton Road, Horsham RH13 5DU.

Finally, thanks to Ebury Press for the use of the photograph shown on p. 31.

First published 1993 by Souvenir Press Ltd,
43 Great Russell Street, London WC1B 3PA
and simultaneously in Canada

ISBN 0 285 63134 9

Typeset by Rowland Phototypesetting Ltd,
Bury St Edmunds, Suffolk

Printed in Italy by
Imago

CONTENTS

INTRODUCTION

In all societies where wedding ceremonies take place, one of the most important aspects of the marriage celebration is the sharing of a wedding feast. Regardless of geography, this very special event in the lives of two people, their families and friends, is commemorated by customs and traditions which are remarkably similar. The feasting and celebration are often marked with the preparation and distribution of an extravagant and spectacular cake, which symbolises the beauty, happiness and prosperity associated with the newly united couple.

On the following pages you will find nine wedding cakes, each prepared and decorated in a different manner, for the purpose of this book is to provide you with the information you need to enable you to reproduce a variety of such cakes in your own kitchen.

Thoughout the book I have been aware of the need to keep things simple, and as far as possible I have tried to ensure that every process is explained in enough detail to allow even the less expert decorator to achieve a satisfactory result. I have learned through many years of teaching and demonstrating that it is vital for every student of sugarcraft to have at least a passing understanding of the basic techniques of applying a coating of icing evenly and neatly. So I have devoted a small amount of space to the two simple skills of applying royal icing and rolled-out icing or sugarpaste. You will find these explanations at the beginning of the section on the first royal iced cake (p. 14) and that for sugarpaste at the beginning of the section on the Spring Tulips cake (p. 40).

All the cakes are graded according to their degree of difficulty, so that you can decide for yourself which are best suited to your experience and natural ability. It is not always the most difficult cakes that are the most impressive, and in fact my favourite cake in this book is actually one of the simplest.

Basic—A relatively easy cake to decorate. Don't be put off even if you have never iced a cake before.

Medium—If you work neatly and have a little cake decorating experience, you should not have much difficulty with this cake. Take it slowly, read the instructions and you will be happy with your results.

Hard—You should have picked up the more specialised skills before attempting this cake. It is assumed that you are already familiar and comfortable with the equipment and the techniques of cake decoration.

The comments above are intended to help you in your choice of cake to decorate. Everyone is different, and what seems easy to one person is difficult to another. Based on my experience as a teacher, the best cake decorators are those who work logically and neatly, taking each process in stages. So, if you really want to make one of the cakes, why not have a go, even if it falls outside your actual level of experience?

I feel it is worth mentioning that whatever elegance the finished cakes and pieces of icing may possess, they have been greatly enhanced by the magic of photography. I am a practical cake decorator and I make mistakes. The secret of good presentation is to disguise them so that they cannot easily be seen. Don't worry if your finished cake has a few imperfections, simply turn those parts towards the back, out of sight!

Royal Iced Roses

Petals of Pastillage

Imperial Splendour

Spring Tulips

Summer Lilies

Autumn Leaves

Winter Wedding

Chocoholic's Dream

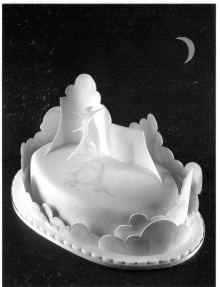

Cloud Nine

We tend to think of the wedding cakes we have seen in sepia-tinted photographs of our parents and grandparents as epitomising the long tradition of the wedding celebration, but in fact these photographs don't take us far enough back to tell anything like the whole story. The history of the wedding cake can be traced beyond the mere introduction of icing to the time when sugar itself was a rare and luxurious commodity. Although it is difficult to believe today, now that sugar has become one of the cheapest ingredients used by the manufacturers of processed foods, there was a time when its use was an expression of privilege, wealth, and extravagance. Natural sugars in the form of syrup, honey and dried fruits were the only sweeteners known to most of the population of Northern Europe, and their inclusion in mediaeval cookery was usually reserved for special occasions.

Cooked mixtures called cakes, for use at marriage festivities, were documented even in Roman times, and the people of Britain in the early Middle Ages were familiar with a cooked delicacy which looked and tasted something like a modern-day oatcake. During the Tudor period the use of this biscuit-like mixture at important events began to reflect the increased sophistication of the times, with the introduction of imported spices and dried fruits brought by merchants trading with the countries of the Eastern Mediterranean area.

Increasing international trade with these countries re-introduced to Britain raisins, dates, and figs, as well as the more exotic flavours of the East. No doubt there were some appalling mistakes as would-be cooks and fashionable bakers experimented with some of the new products for the first time. We can safely guess that the early attempts to mix them with traditional ingredients such as minced meat would be highly unpalatable to modern tastes.

The recipe for wedding cake as we know it today began to emerge in the seventeenth century. Its basis was a plum cake, although to modern eyes it would still have been no more than an especially rich bread. It was primarily a flour and yeast mix, spiced with small quantities of butter, milk, sugar, eggs, and currants. The earliest recipe known to be associated with a wedding was published in 1655 and was described as a Banbury cake. Subsequently the flour lost its predominance, the eggs began to be included in quantity and gradually replaced yeast as the raising agent, and other dried fruits, candied peels, almonds and alcohol came to be incorporated in varying proportions. It was necessary to confine this less solid mixture, or batter, inside a hoop or tin in order to bake it, and by the mid-eighteenth century the plum cake had finally established itself. It was the forerunner of the twentieth-century rich fruit cake.

We owe the first published recipe for a 'Bride Cake' to a Manchester confectioner, Mrs Elizabeth Raffald, whose book, when it finally went out of print in 1825, had indelibly established the basic wedding cake recipe for other experts to copy and refine. The notable feature of Mrs Raffald's cake was not so much the ingredients as her instructions for covering the cake first with almond icing, and then with a white icing made with egg white and powdered sugar. The 'double coating' was a new variation of two older and separate techniques: of covering cakes with almond pastes, and of glazing them with powdered sugar and beaten egg white.

This idea did not really catch on for another century, however, even though by the 1830s some fashionable Edinburgh confectioners were colouring icing for bride cakes with cochineal to produce pink cakes, and even decorating them with sugar paste motifs, and emblems such as cupids, cherubs and doves.

During the mid-nineteenth century, especially at around the time of the Great Exhibition of 1851, Britain grew to new heights of wealth and imperial splendour. The feeling of national confidence this created was reflected in almost all aspects of fashionable life, including the quest for novel and spectacular ways of presenting food. Bride cakes became taller and taller, supporting amazing superstructures made from sugarpaste. Cakes were piled one upon another and bore pastillage models of classical statues, flags of the Empire, commemorative scenes, flowers and foliage, all made from sugar.

Slightly later came another development in icing techniques—that of piping. This skill, introduced from the continent, was enthusiastically adopted in the 1890s as it permitted elaborate and repetitive forms of ornamentation to be applied in patterns which have since become associated with the wedding cake. Piped birds, bunches of grapes, baskets and trellises became so commonplace a form of decoration on the typical wedding cake that the work was often left to the apprentices, and until the early 1980s cakes for weddings relied on the techniques which had evolved almost a hundred years earlier.

The increasing cost of labour, and the diminishing number of master confectioners with icing skills, halted the development and evolution of wedding cake decorating. However, things had been happening overseas, in other English-speaking parts of the world, especially in Australia and South Africa. There the tradition of ornate wedding cakes was adapted to cope with the extremes of warmer, more humid climates, and in the early 1980s inexpensive soft icing mixes used for coating cakes were quickly and successfully introduced to Britain from Australia and South Africa. These sugar pastes caught the bakery trade unawares, and for several years the development of new and exciting styles of wedding cake decoration, incorporating beautifully crafted sugar flowers and very fine piping and linework, was left to enthusiastic amateurs.

Indeed, the finest practitioners of the skill of cake decorating are now virtually all amateurs, and cake decorating has become an art form and a fascinating hobby for literally thousands of people worldwide.

The organisation of even a simple wedding is a complicated business, involving the co-ordination of many separate elements; even if you are able to delegate much of the work to others, you will still want to supervise the arrangements to ensure that nothing has been overlooked.

If you are organising the wedding cake you can avoid unnecessary difficulties by following the countdown set out below. So long as you adhere to the approximate timings suggested, you will find that the completion of your cake is comparatively trouble-free, and as the work progresses it will even provide you with pleasure and an opportunity to escape from the pressures building up elsewhere.

Several months before the wedding you are likely to have a reasonable idea of how many guests you will be catering for at the reception, so you can start to plan the size of cake you require. The simplest shape for those who will have to cut it into portions is a square one. However, if you are decorating it yourself, it is worth noting that the easiest cakes to ice, whether using sugarpaste or royal icing, are round.

In order to estimate how large the cake should be, or how many tiers you will need, remember that when caterers cut portions for guests, they cut comparatively small slices. Each piece is usually a finger of cake about an inch square, not a wedge-shaped slice. In theory, therefore, a square cake baked in a 25cm (10in) tin will yield one hundred portions. In practice you should allow for wastage, and it is safer to assume that such a cake will give you about eighty to ninety pieces. A reference table suggesting the approximate number of portions provided from most cakes is provided on p. 95.

Don't forget that you will probably want to send portions to those relatives and friends unable to attend the wedding, so you should include them in your calculations. Some families like to have an extra tier, and deliberately choose a cake which is larger than the minimum required. Many newly married couples also like to retain the smallest tier complete, since it will last for up to two years if it is correctly stored, and may then be used for a christening or anniversary celebration.

At the planning stage you may also take the opportunity to select the type of cake. It doesn't have to be a rich celebration cake, full of fruit and peel. It is perfectly acceptable to make one using a madeira or genoese recipe, a chocolate cake, a cherry cake or a combination of any of these.

You will have to pay attention to the physical size of a baked sponge, however, since you will want to provide your guests with larger slices of a sponge than you would of a fruit cake. There is a cutting chart for sponge cakes on p. 95. If you do mix the recipes, ensure that the heavier, more substantial portion made with a traditional fruit cake recipe forms the lower part of a tiered cake.

A rich fruit cake improves with age, and a really fresh one, eaten within a day or so of baking, is not as tasty as one three or four months old. So if you choose to use the traditional celebration fruit cake, begin your preparation early. If you are going to bake a sponge, a madeira or genoese, for example, wait until seven to ten days before the wedding day before you begin your baking, or bake it early and freeze it.

Here is the countdown in detail if you are making a traditional rich fruit cake.

4 MONTHS before the wedding

Having decided on the sizes and shapes of the individual tiers of the cake, buy or arrange to hire the necessary baking tins from a specialised cake decorations shop. You can also hire a variety of cakestands. There are very traditional round or square silver bases which support tiered cakes, acrylic plastic stands which are assembled in a variety of configurations depending on the nature of the cakes, and elegant chromed stands designed to make the cake tiers appear to be floating on air.

Purchase all the dried fruit, the peel, the currants, sultanas and raisins, and wash the fruit thoroughly—especially the currants since even if they are labelled as having been washed, you'll be surprised at how much extra grit you extract. Dry all the fruit, stir it together in a large bowl and soak it with a cupful of alcohol such as rum or sherry or, if you prefer, orange juice. If you seal the bowl with clingfilm you can leave the fruit for several days, only disturbing it to give it an occasional stirring. The longer you leave the fruit the more it 'plumps up', ensuring a moist cake.

The day before you bake the cakes, put out the butter and eggs you intend to use in the mixture in order to bring them to room temperature.

Line the tins with brown paper, strong greaseproof, or a teflon-coated non-stick baking cloth cut to size.

Rich fruit cakes benefit from slow baking at a low temperature, so make sure that if you are cooking a large tier, which may take up to six hours, you arrange things so that it finishes cooking at a convenient time. Unless you are very practised, it is helpful to check the cake an hour or so before you expect it to be ready, by piercing it in the centre with a smooth metal meat skewer. When the cake surface is evenly baked to a rich chestnut-brown colour, you should try the skewer test. Push the skewer in and immediately withdraw it. If there is any cake mix sticking to the metal, leave it in the oven for a further half hour, and test again. It is ready when the skewer emerges from the centre of the cake clean and shiny. A further useful indication that the cake is properly cooked right through is to tap it gently with the fingers. If you hear a slightly hollow sound, you can be sure that the mixture has risen evenly, at which point it should be taken from the oven and allowed to cool overnight, before removing it from the tin. Do not, at this stage, take off its lining paper. Simply wrap the cake in greaseproof, and then a layer of cooking foil, and store it in a cool place. Don't put it in the freezer as this will impede its maturing process.

3 MONTHS to go

Confirm the colour scheme for the wedding, the details of the flowers and the dresses of the bridesmaids. If the cake is to be decorated with sprays of sugar flowers, start making them. Any piped off-pieces, sugar or pastillage ornaments or sugar lace can be made and stored in a cardboard box in a dry place. Do not put them in an airtight box or they may become soft.

2 MONTHS to go

Purchase the cake boards. They are usually 1cm (½in) thick and coated with silver paper. They can be purchased in sizes increasing in 2.5cm (1in) increments, up to 45cm (18in) across. If you are not sure what size cake boards you need, make a note of the tin sizes you used for baking the cakes, and follow the rule that each cake needs a board at least 5cm (2in) bigger. If the cake is tiered, the base tier is usually on a board 10cm (4in) larger than the cake resting on it.

You can also obtain cake boxes, pillars if required, icing sugar, marzipan and prepared sugarpaste. Ready-made sugarpaste icing is available in a wide variety of pastel hues and a few primary colours, which can be mixed together to create special shades, so it may be helpful to take a small colour sample along to the shop where you make your purchases.

6 WEEKS to go

Marzipan the cakes and put them in their cardboard cake boxes. Keep them at room temperature and leave them for a week.

5 WEEKS to go

Cover the cakes with royal icing or sugarpaste, and if you are going to crimp or inlay a pattern, do it immediately you have covered the cakes. Put them back in their boxes and leave them for another week for the icing to harden off.

4 WEEKS to go

Prepare all the patterns and scribe them onto the icing. Pipe all the decorations.

3 WEEKS to go

Prepare templates and position pillars on the cakes so that the flower sprays or decorations can be assembled and arranged. Attach any off-pieces, like sugar lace or the coronets which are part of the decoration.

2 WEEKS to go

Assemble the cake on a level surface and make any adjustments. This is the time for family and close friends to have a look at it and perhaps take some photographs. If it is to be transported to a wedding reception it is helpful to lay a piece of thin foam sponge in the base of each of the cake boxes before packing the cakes. This helps cushion any vibration and also prevents the cake board from sliding around.

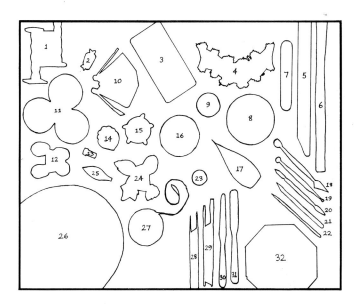

CAKE DECORATING EQUIPMENT

1. **Pink and white spiral twisted wedding cake pillars**
2. **Two star-shaped calyx cutters**
3. **Easyflow icing smoother**
4. **Six assorted bundles artificial stamens**
5. **Straight edge for smoothing royal icing**
6. **Green florist's wire**
7. **Mini-rolling pin (15cm non-stick nylon)**
8. **Set of plastic circular cutters**
9. **Set of two plastic serrated rose leaf cutters**
10. **Three mini-crimpers (for patterning sugarpaste)**
11. **Three bowls of dusting colour**
12. **Assorted pots of concentrated paste colours**
13. **Pot of gold flake (real gold leaf in tiny pieces)**
14. **Set of two orchid cutters (for orchid throat)**
15. **Maple leaf cutter**
16. **Garrett frill cutter with interchangeable centre cutter**
17. **Three large leaf cutters**
18. **Shell and blade modelling tool**
19. **Ball tool**
20. **Fluted cone tool**
21. **Scalpel**
22. **Stainless steel scriber**
23. **Broderie anglaise cutter**
24. **Four assorted leaf-veining tools**
25. **Pair of lily petal cutters**
26. **Icing turntable**
27. **Roll of green florist's tape**
28. **Two sable paint brushes**
29. **Two nylon dusting brushes**
30. **Cranked palette knife (10cm blade)**
31. **Straight-bladed palette knife**
32. **Foam Hexipad for flowers**

ROYAL ICED ROSES

Items needed to make this cake:

15cm (6in) rich round fruit cake
23cm (9in) rich round fruit cake
30cm (12in) rich round fruit cake
23cm (9in) round silver cake board and white
    wedding cake box
30cm (12in) round silver cake board and white
    wedding cake box
38cm (15in) round silver cake board and white
    wedding cake box
3 × 7.5cm (3in) silver hexagonal pillars
4 × 9cm (3½in) silver hexagonal pillars (one for the
    vase)
3 metres of 1cm wide silver paper board banding
Spray of artificial silk flowers for top tier
41cm (16in) stainless steel straight edge
Stainless steel side scraper
Writing nozzles—Nos. 1, 2, 3
Rope nozzles—Nos. 44, 43
Leaf nozzle—No. 50
Parchment triangles
Non-stick Quickslip sheet or waxed paper
Paint brushes
Peach concentrated paste food colouring
Moss green concentrated paste food colouring
3kg (6lb) royal icing
3kg (6lb) white almond marzipan
Glycerine
Piped sugar roses—minimum of 18 Large, 36
                Medium, 72 Small, and 44 Buds
Piped sugar doves—minimum of 36

I like variety in my cake decorating designs, and for the first wedding cake in this book I have combined royal icing in warm peach and apricot shades with silk flowers.

This style of icing has several practical advantages over more extreme designs, not the least being that the finished product is quite robust. Since many cakes have to be transported over long distances in order to set them up at wedding receptions, this is no small consideration. The piped decorations are strongly made and protected by large cake boards which greatly assist in preventing damage to the ornamentation. Another advantage of this cake is that because of its regular shape it is easy to cut, without undue wastage.

It is also capable of being stored for many months, and the smallest tier with its top ornament is entirely appropriate for an anniversary celebration or even a christening.

Marzipan the cake one week prior to coating it

1. **The top rim of the cake is edged with a sausage of marzipan, so that when the cake is eventually inverted, this sausage forms a good seal between the cake and its board. Roll out the marzipan for the cake top. Brush it with piping gel, and lay the cake onto it. Trim off the excess and when the cake is turned over the marzipan will provide a completely flat surface ready for icing.**

2. **A strip of marzipan is rolled out until it is a little wider than the height of the cake and about three times its diameter. The edges of the strip are trimmed, and it is brushed with piping gel. Then the cake is rolled onto the 'bandage' of marzipan.**

with royal icing. Begin by rolling out sufficient marzipan to cover it with a thickness of between 2.5 and 5mm (⅜ and ¼in). To estimate the quantity required, weigh your cake, and take half of that weight, e.g. 3kg (6lb) cake = 1.5kg (3lb) marzipan.

At first, roll the marzipan to thin it, but to obtain an even thickness, grip the ends of the pin and 'skid' it lightly over the surface. You will feel the bumps smooth out.

Use the tin in which you baked the cake as a pattern to cut out the correct sized area of marzipan for the cake top. Trim surplus from the top by holding the knife at an acute angle to the side of the cake.

ROYAL ICING

Royal icing is used for all piping—for making shells, embroidery, lace and extension. It is important especially for fine work to have freshly beaten royal icing if you are to achieve the best results.

Working with royal icing is the single most important aspect of cake decorating. It is made by beating together sugar and egg whites. The action of beating incorporates millions of minute air bubbles into the mixture, and it is these which give it its texture. The slightest trace of egg yolk or grease, however, will prevent it from becoming properly aerated, so always use scrupulously clean utensils. Mixing bowls of glass, copper or stainless steel are best for making icing in.

The whites of eggs moisten the powdered sugar as well as aerating it, and it is a good idea to break and separate the eggs you are going to use well in advance. This will allow some of the water to evaporate from the white, which increases its viscosity and ultimately makes a stronger icing.

TO MAKE ROYAL ICING BY HAND

1 egg white—break the egg the night before, leave covered at room temperature as it produces a better volume and beats more easily.

Icing sugar—about 375g (12oz) (the amount used

3. **Be sure that the icing is well mixed immediately before you apply it. Make it at least a day in advance, and stir it gently before use. Place the cake on a revolving turntable and use a broad-bladed palette knife to transfer the icing to it.**

will depend on the size of the egg white). Make sure the icing sugar is sieved through a fine sieve at the time you are making up the royal icing.

Lemon juice—strained—the amount depending on how much royal icing is to be made up. Lemon juice is an acetic acid and it will whiten your icing and give it elasticity, but if too much is added it will cause the icing to become brittle when dry.

Place the egg white into a bowl and gradually add the icing sugar about a dessertspoon at a time, beating well after each addition. Make sure that, as it is added, you stir round the sides of the bowl and regularly clean the blade of your knife on the edge of the bowl. Do not be tempted to add too much icing sugar too quickly—you will simply make heavy, 'dead' icing which will be very hard after it has dried.

Continue adding icing sugar until the mixture is of a thick consistency and firm enough to hold a peak. Add a few drops of lemon juice through a strainer, and the icing will become softer and creamier, and develop a silky sheen. Stir it carefully, and put it to one side, covered with a damp cloth.

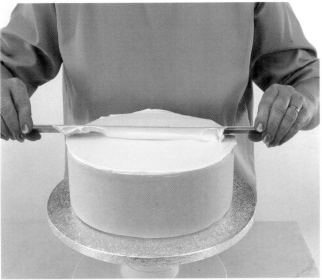

4. 'Paddle' the icing with the flat of the knife blade. Use a side-to-side movement to spread it evenly by slowly rotating the turntable as you work the knife. Press quite hard to burst any air bubbles and do not expect to complete the coating with only one layer. You will require at least three to build up a smooth finish.

5. A metal straight edge is used to smooth the icing. Start at the far side of the cake and, holding the straight edge at both ends, draw it towards you. Turn it over so that the other edge is in the icing, and push it steadily back to its starting point. Note how, by turning it over, the icing only builds up against one face of the tool.

TO MAKE ROYAL ICING BY MACHINE

Using powdered albumen to make up royal icing:
Mix together:

	SMALL AMOUNT	MEDIUM AMOUNT	LARGE AMOUNT
Albumen	15g (½oz)	45g (1½oz)	85g (3oz)
Water	90ml (3fl oz)	285ml (10fl oz) ½pt	567ml (20fl oz) 1pt
Icing sugar	454g (1lb)	1kg 590g (3½lb)	3.174kg (7lb)

When making royal icing it is important to be accurate with weighing your ingredients. With recipes for cakes, etc., it is perfectly acceptable to round the weights up or down to the figures given.

When the powdered egg albumen is added to the water, the mixture appears very lumpy at first. Stir it with a fork, then let it rest for a few minutes. Return to it and stir it again every five minutes. After about half an hour the mixture will be free from lumps.

The albumen solution will keep up to one week before the addition of icing sugar, but powdered albumen will keep for many months, so it is not necessary to mix it all at once.

Sieve 454g (1lb) icing sugar into the bowl, pour the solution through a sieve, set the machine on its lowest speed and mix for about 15 minutes. Once the icing has reached a soft peak consistency, put it into a clean, dry, airtight container, covering the surface of the icing with a little clingfilm before sealing. This prevents air from crusting the sugar.

If royal icing is to be used only for coating the cake, weigh out the correct amount into a clean bowl, and then add 1 teaspoon of glycerine to each 500g (1lb). This will make a slightly softer icing which is easier to cut. However, glycerine is hydroscopic and it draws moisture from the atmosphere, or even from the marzipan and cake. In time this may cause the icing to turn yellow.

Invert sugar is more effective than glycerine as it is not hydroscopic, but it is quite difficult to obtain, even from large chemist's shops.

6. Allow the top to dry for 24 hours, then trim any projecting lumps from around the edge, and apply icing to the sides with a palette knife. Paddle well to distribute the icing evenly over the sides and to eliminate any air bubbles.

7. Smooth it with a stainless steel side scraper, by rotating the turntable while holding the scraper at an angle of about 30 degrees to the side of the cake. Move it onto the icing and turn the cake through a full circle in a single steady movement. Hold the scraper stationary and move the cake.

8. After three layers of icing, the next step is to coat the cake board. You can use a palette knife to smooth it out—as well as making a clean-looking finish at the base of your cake, it hides any marks that you might have made on the board while coating the sides.

9. Piping icing is easiest when you put it into small, disposable bags made from vegetable parchment. The advantage is that you can hold a small bag easily in the hand, and throw it away when it is empty. This is how to fold a bag, starting with a triangular-shaped piece of parchment.

PIPING

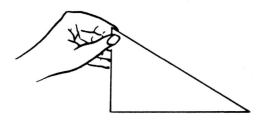

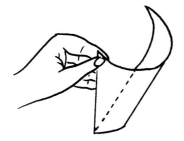

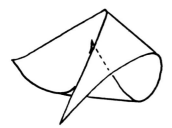

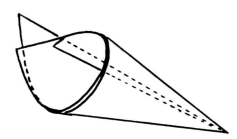

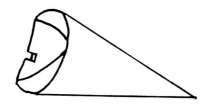

10. When the paper cone has been drawn tight, it has a sharp point at its tip. Notice how the corner of the triangle in the right hand has been pulled towards the dotted line. The point of the bag can be cut off, and a metal icing nozzle placed inside before it is filled with icing.

11. You will need as much icing as you can scoop up on the blade of a palette knife. If you are working with very small icing nozzles, one bag may have sufficient icing in it to last for several hours, so it is best to use piping bags made with good-quality vegetable parchment because they do not split during use.

PIPING LINES

Hold the bag and the nozzle at 45° angle. Touch the surface where the line is to be started and squeeze the back of the bag gently to attach the icing to the surface. Lift the tube whilst steadily applying pressure, and extend a thread of icing to the length required. Stop pressing, and at the same time bring the nozzle down to touch the surface. Lift the nozzle away.

PIPING SHELLS AND STARS

To use a star nozzle, hold the icing bag at 45° angle. Touch the surface lightly with the nozzle, squeeze and allow the icing to build up to the required size, pull nozzle away. To pipe a border, remember not to pipe the stars too close together or their shape will be lost.

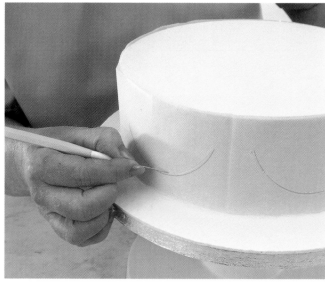

12. Transfer the designs to the side of the cake by scratching through the paper pattern with a scriber. You only need to establish a bare outline of the design, since once the most important features are in place, you can fill in the complete pattern with the icing itself. The pattern to be traced is on p. 21.

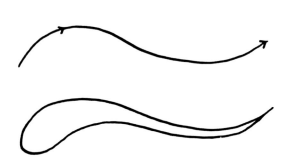

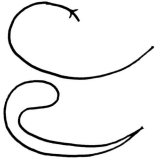

13. Making shells, scrolls and stars uses more icing, so a larger bag is required. These stars are made with a No. 44 nozzle. The icing is squeezed out until a large serrated ball is formed. The pressure on the bag is released and the tip is withdrawn. Keep the tip of the nozzle clean by wiping it regularly with a damp cloth.

14. The pattern is emphasised with scrolls piped over and around the stars. They are piped with a No. 43, and raised to greater prominence by overpiping them with a line piped with a No. 3. On the finished cake it will be seen that yet another line has been added using a No. 2 nozzle, for more emphasis.

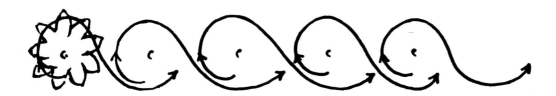

15. The upper edges of the cake are piped with an S scroll—using a No. 43. Heavy pressure on the bag forms the beginning of the scroll, then the pressure is reduced as the nozzle is moved along the curve. The pressure is released altogether as it reaches the tail. The scroll is overpiped using the same nozzle but with a steady pressure.

16. To emphasise the shape of the S scroll, it is again overpiped with a No. 3 nozzle and then a No. 2. Try to ensure that every scroll is the same size.

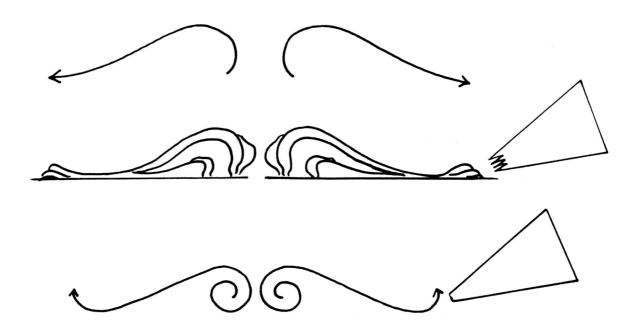

17. Throughout the book there are references to icing nozzles and piping bags, and these are the ones used. There are others available for specific purposes, but you will find that those listed below are essential:

Writing—No. 0, 1, 2, 3, 4
Star—No. 5
Rope—No. 44, 43
Petal—No. 58
Basket/Frill—No. 19B
Leaf—No. 50.
The icing nozzle brush is vital for cleaning the delicate tips.

DOVES AND ROSES

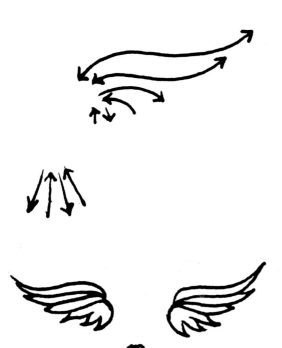

Doves—actual size

18. The wings and tail feathers of the dove are piped as individual pieces, each using a No. 1 icing nozzle. Pipe them on teflon-coated Quickslip cloth, so that they will dry quickly and release easily. Follow the diagram on this page.

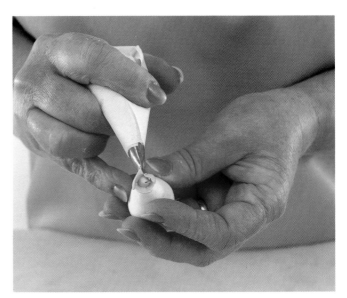

21. These piped flowers are made on the tip of a sugarpaste cone. A No. 58 petal nozzle is used. Place the nozzle against the top of the cone with the thin end of the nozzle pointing inwards and upwards. A fine cylinder of icing is formed as the cone is rotated. Three petals are piped in a clockwise direction just below it, with each one slightly overlapping its neighbour.

19. When dry, they are lifted from the cloth and inserted into a freshly piped teardrop of royal icing. The tail is inserted between the wings at the pointed end of the teardrop. They are very light and will stay in place without support.

20. The head and beak are piped onto the body, and the bird is left to dry. Doves are delicate decorations, which look good on most types of wedding cake. The wings of the doves have all been dusted with apricot petal dust before securing them with a little royal icing.

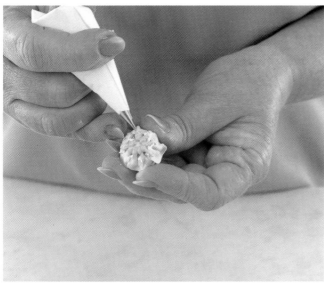

22. The next step is to pipe another row of three. This time rotate the cone in the opposite direction, so that the overlapping part of each petal is on the opposite edge to those in the previous row. Repeat this step several times, on each occasion reversing the rotation of the work and making the petals larger.

23. When dry, the rose is cut from its cone, and a calyx is piped onto the back. Roses may be stored indefinitely by placing them in a foam sponge-lined box, and keeping them in a dry cupboard. Stick them in place using a leaf nozzle and a little green royal icing. The smallest rosebuds are at each end of the scallop, and the largest are in the centre.

PETALS OF PASTILLAGE

Items needed to make this cake:

20cm (8in) rich fruit cake
30cm (12in) rich fruit cake
28cm (11in) round silver cake board
41cm (16in) round silver cake board
13cm (5in) acrylic tube
No. 2 writing nozzle
No. 4 writing nozzle
Eyelet cutter
Small leaf cutter
Set of 2 large petal cutters
Set of 5 lily cutters
Piece of corrugated DIY plastic sheeting
2 metres of 1cm wide white ribbon for board edging
Stainless steel straight edge
Stainless steel smoother
Parchment triangles
Paint brush
2.25kg (4.5lb) white marzipan
2kg (4lb) white royal icing
1kg (2lb) white pastillage or Petal Paste
Emery boards
Small pieces of foam sponge
Four containers ranging in size from a petit-four case to 10cm (4in) to set centre flower in.

A simple cake, plainly coated with royal icing, and embellished with petals made from pastillage, is an impressive centrepiece on the wedding table.

Pastillage or gum paste has been familiar to Italian confectioners for centuries, and by the turn of this century many English craftsmen were making a large range of gum paste ornaments, flowers and leaves for wedding and other celebration cakes. They kept a large stock of moulds and formers which regrettably were lost to the trade after they were superseded by mass-produced china ornaments.

There are many old recipes for the preparation of pastillage or gum paste, although they nearly all contain a mixture of gum tragacanth, icing sugar and cornflour.

Gum tragacanth can be purchased from most cake decorating shops in a white powder form and is used for adding strength to gum paste or pastillage. An instant pastillage powder called Petal Paste is available.

The two-tier cake shown here can be decorated over a period of only four days, including the royal icing for coating the cake. It is even quicker if it uses sugarpaste.

The secret of its speedy completion is the accurate measurement of the off-pieces—the outer ring of petals—since they must be the correct width when they are attached to the cake, or a gap will be left when the last one is placed in position.

It is possible to avoid the need for complicated arithmetic by cutting a circle of exactly the diameter of the iced cake from a piece of paper, folding it into quarters, then folding it twice more, so that when opened up it is creased into sixteen wedge-shaped segments. The widest point of each wedge is the width of each of the sixteen leaves needed.

Each leaf is cut using the larger of the two petal cutters and then perforated using a broderie anglaise cutter and a small leaf cutter. It is then draped over a sheet of corrugated plastic roofing material from a DIY store, and allowed to dry.

The process is repeated for the upper tier using the smaller petal cutter which is also used for those on the inner support between the tiers. Because the supporting column is comparatively small, only twelve leaves are needed to surround it.

Helpful hint: The experts say that corrugated plastic sheeting can be cut very easily with a saw. In my experience this is not so, as it splinters and shatters. The practical solution is to cut it with a pair of strong kitchen scissors. It is slow work, but not as difficult as the alternative of sawing it, and there are fewer broken bits to sweep up!

The waterlily on the top tier is formed by arranging six of the smallest petals in a petit-four case which has royal icing piped into the base. When dry they are transferred to a silicone-paper cake case. A ring of icing is piped around the centre petals, and eight of the larger petals are inserted to form a ring around the six central ones. Leave them to dry before removing the cake case.

Continue to enlarge the centrepiece with another two rows of petals (10 of the next size petal for row 3 and 11 of the second largest size for row 4). Use a slightly larger container for each row.

You could modify this design by adding colour to the flower. Start off with the centre petals in a deep pink, and make each subsequent row a slightly paler shade. This technique is very useful if you wish to co-ordinate the colour scheme of the bride's accessories with the cake design.

PETAL CUTTERS

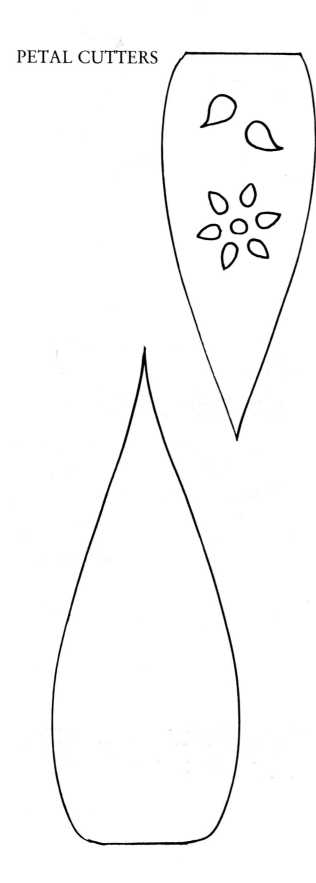

1. **When cutting the petals, make one which you can use as a guide. Cut all the subsequent ones to match it. In particular make sure that the cut-out flower patterns are in the same place on each one.**

4. **Assembling the tiers is simple. The petals are stuck around a column of 13cm-diameter plastic tubing, cut to be 2.5cm taller than the length of the pastillage pieces. Apply a small amount of icing to the base of the tube and set it in place. Then attach the petals by piping a small amount of icing to the base of each one, and to the part where it will touch the tubing.**

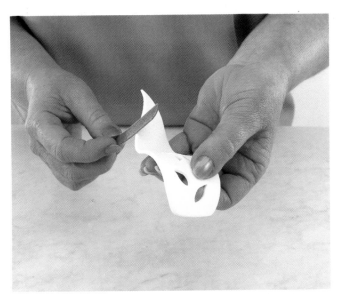

2. As each petal is completed, lay it across the ridges of a piece of corrugated plastic. To make certain that every petal has the same curvature, rule guide marks on the underside of the plastic and align the ends of the petals to the marks.

3. Make all the petals at the same time. It takes about 24 hours for them to dry really hard. Smooth and trim the edges by sanding away any burrs with a manicurist's emery board. Pastillage is brittle, so work very carefully, supporting it close to the area you are trimming.

5. Make the flower by arranging five or six of the smallest petals in a very small container and sticking them together with royal icing. A foil chocolate case is ideal for this stage. In this illustration the second row of petals is being added. This time a paper baking case is all that is needed to hold them while the icing dries.

6. Use whatever container you can find in the kitchen to set subsequent rows of petals in. A flan cutter is good because it is very shallow, and can be easily removed.

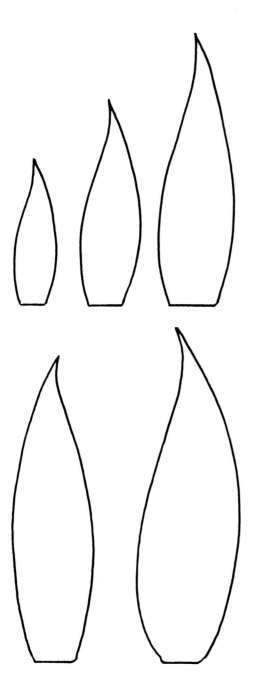

7. The half-finished flower is very fragile, so take great care as you stick it to the cake with a dab of royal icing. If you have the misfortune to break a leaf, you can repair it with icing, but you will have to support it on a pad until it dries.

10. The cake rapidly assumes its finished form when the side pieces are added. Secure them with two dabs of icing, one at the centre and one at the base of each petal.

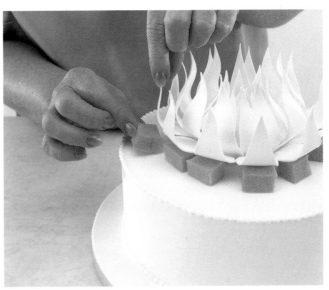

8. A row of beading is piped around the rim of the cake using a No. 3 icing nozzle. Make sure that the icing beads are regularly spaced and equal in size.

9. The last row of petals is added and glued in place with more royal icing. Each petal rests on its own foam sponge support while the icing hardens.

11. Each petal is laid carefully into position. You will need up to 20 petals for each tier, although it is a sensible precaution to make a few extra ones to allow for any breakages.

12. With any simple design, it is essential to keep your work very tidy. Use a soft brush to wipe away any excess icing from around the edges of the petals.

IMPERIAL SPLENDOUR

Items needed to make this cake:

2 × 15cm (6in) round rich fruit cakes 7.5cm (3in) high
3 × 23cm (9in) round rich fruit cakes 7.5cm (3in) high
3 × 30cm (12in) round rich fruit cakes 10cm (4in) high
1 × 15cm (6in) round thin cake card
2 × 23cm (9in) round thin cake cards
2 × 30cm (12in) round thin cake cards
20cm (8in) round thick cake board for top tier
23cm (9in) round thick cake board for top tier
28cm (11in) round thick cake board for middle tier
30cm (12in) round thick cake board for middle tier
36cm (14in) round thick cake board for bottom tier
41cm (16in) round thick cake board for bottom tier
46cm (18in) round thick cake board for bottom tier
10cm (4in) polystyrene disk 2.5cm (1in) high
20cm (8in) polystyrene disk 5cm (2in) high
Writing nozzles—1, 1.5, 2, 3, 4
Shell nozzles—5, 6, 8
Rope nozzles—42, 43, 44
Leaf nozzles—50, 51, 52
Small and large parchment triangles
Non-stick Quickslip sheet
Nylon piping bag
Nozzle adaptor
Vase mould
3.5 metres cream-coloured lace for board edging
7kg (15lb) white almond marzipan
4kg (8lb) royal icing
500g (1lb) Petal Paste pastillage

With its exuberant celebration of the skills of piping in royal icing, the cake illustrated in the following pages has provided me with a host of anecdotes, many of which I would never have expected when I set out to design it. Many of them fall into the 'Blimey, it ain't 'arf big' school of thought, and although widely appreciated by elderly bakers who spent the best years of their young lives making similar cakes, some may feel that the style is too formal. If you like it, however, read on, because although superficially daunting it is not as difficult to make as it looks. It is repetitive, though, and it will take you about sixty hours to pipe and apply all the decorations.

The Victorians discovered that the secret of making really tall cakes was to pile one on top of another, and that is what has been done here. The lower sections are made of three cakes, each coated with marzipan, and then placed together and re-iced in order to give the drum shape a smooth vertical surface.

Since this calls for a large and robust tilting turntable, you could achieve the same visual effect, albeit with fewer portions of cake, by joining together two or three polystyrene cake dummies, icing them as described on the following pages, and using the artificial cake as a platform for the smaller edible cake. This is not cheating, it is a standard practice which is used regularly by professional caterers when they need to achieve a theatrical effect.

Each layer of cake is positioned on a card and small horizontal reference marks are made on the coating icing. It is clear from their position where the layers begin underneath the icing. This permits the upper sections to be more easily dismantled without damaging the entire cake.

THE DESIGN

The patterns piped onto the sides of this cake are repeated six times on each tier. The same design is used throughout, and it is reproduced at a suitable scale to suit the proportions of each cake. The diagrams on p. 39 indicate that two stages are involved. The basic piping is shown in the first example, and the finishing embellishments in the second. The first step is to scratch the design onto the cake with a metal scriber. Mark only the outline to show the general position of the main decoration. Transfer the design to a tracing paper template, and then have it photocopied to the correct proportions for each of the cakes to avoid the necessity for reproducing it manually.

This is a cake in a classic style, and the base of each tier is bevelled at an angle of about 30 degrees, by placing the cake on two cake boards, the first of which is about 5cm (2in) larger than the cake, and the second about 10cm (4in) larger. For an even deeper bevel, it may be necessary to add a third board 15cm (6in) bigger than the cake. The area around the boards is completely encased in royal icing. To obtain an even finish, it will be necessary to apply up to three coats, allowing each to dry overnight before applying the next.

In the illustrations shown I am working on the middle tier, but the method of icing is the same for each. Keep all the patterns in proportion by using the larger nozzles on the bottom tier—a No. 4 is

used on the lowest tier, and to pipe the same design a No. 3 is used for the middle tier, and a No. 2 for the top tier.

The three tiers are separated by shallow discs which have been made by applying a coating of royal icing to polystyrene dummies. It is vital to ensure that the tops of each cake are exactly horizontal, so check them on a flat surface, using a spirit level, and if there is a slight deviation, correct it with a packing of icing. If you fail to do this, your cake will be unstable when you finally assemble it.

1. This kind of icing uses the principle of building up a series of piped lines in order to achieve extra depth in the pattern. With the larger patterns such as the long vase and the deep V shown here, begin work with a No. 3 icing nozzle.

4. The leaves are piped using a special nozzle which has a slit at its tip; it is used by touching the cake with the top of the tube and, while maintaining a constant pressure on the icing bag, jiggling the tube up and down to crinkle the leaf. When the pressure is eased, the tube is pulled gently away from the cake, leaving a leaf-shaped deposit of icing.

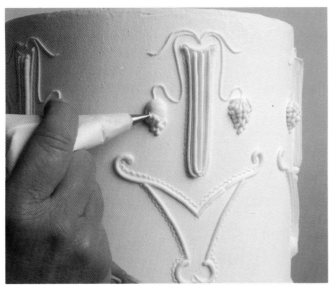

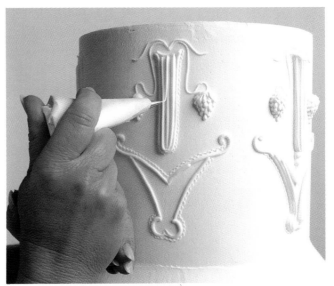

2. Grapes are piped in two stages. Start by piping a large teardrop shape using a No. 4 nozzle. When it is dry, begin at the lowest part with a No. 3 nozzle and pipe a series of small teardrops. They are piped in rows, and the 'tail' of each droplet is hidden beneath the body of the one just above it.

3. The parallel lines inside the long vases are piped as 3 lines with a No. 4 nozzle—then all the lines, including the outer ones, are overpiped with Nos. 2, 1.5 and 1. Apply four lines to each section, waiting for one line to dry before piping the next directly over it. The scallop around the V-shaped hollow-stem piping is made with a No. 1.

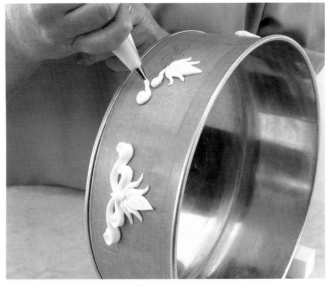

5. Hollow stem piping. By building up a series of slightly offset lines overpiped with a No. 2 nozzle, it is possible to create a hollow shell. Work alternately first one side, then on the other, bringing the pairs of lines closer to one another until it is possible to link them with a single line. If there are any open areas at the point where lines change direction fill them in with a neat row of teardrops.

6. The six coronets arranged around the top are piped over the side of the tins used for baking the cakes. They dry into a curve which closely matches that of the cake, thus making them easy to fit. The centre parts are piped with a No. 3 nozzle and then a No. 1. The scrolls to the left and right, are piped with a No. 43, and then overpiped with a No. 2.

HANDLE-SHAPED BRACKETS

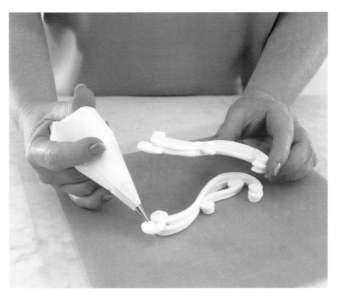

7. The handle-shaped brackets set on the top edge of the cake are piped onto a non-stick sheet. Tape it over with the template showing a silhouette of the bracket. Pipe a thick line directly over the small S-shaped part, then pipe the longer section. Use a No. 43 or 44 depending on the tier. Overpipe with a No. 3, and then a No. 2. Each bracket is piped in two halves.

8. When dry remove each pair from the non-stick sheet and use royal icing to join them. A damp paint brush drawn along the join line between the halves will remove any excess icing squeezed from the joint.

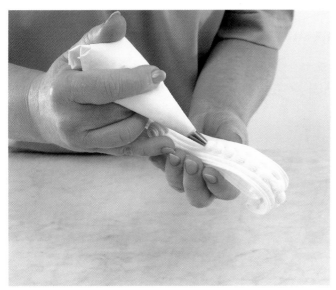

9. Since the curves are piped freehand, it is possible that the two halves may not match precisely. However it is possible to disguise any imperfections and enhance the design at the same time, by piping a continuous overlapping row of shells across the join, with the No. 44 nozzle.

10. Brackets and the coronets are held in place with yet more icing. It is recommended that these pieces are positioned after all other work on the cake is completed, as they project from the cake and may suffer accidental damage through careless handling.

THE VASE

I have made the pastillage vase in a hand-made clay mould, and brief instructions for making a mould follow. However, if you prefer, a vase filled with a small spray of flowers or a ceramic statuette is equally suitable and attractive.

To make a sugar vase similar to that illustrated, it is first necessary to make a female mould from a china or porcelain vase using modelling clay. Make two half-moulds and remove them from the original before the clay sets. Because they should be fairly

strong, build them up to a thickness of about 1cm (½in), and let the clay dry out for about 72 hours before attempting to use them.

Support the halves while they are drying, or there is a risk that they will distort. Then paint the inside with varnish or emulsion paint to seal the surface. This will allow the pastillage pieces to be released easily when you use the mould for the first time.

Trim off any ragged edges and fit the two halves together to ensure that they make a close fit. If there are any gaps, smooth along the join with coarse sandpaper.

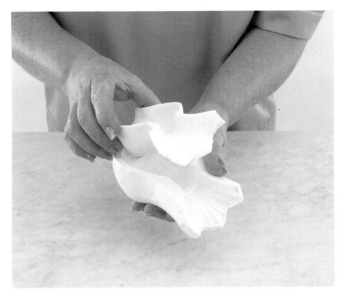

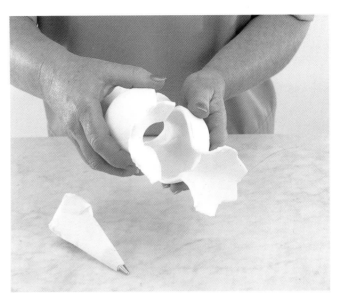

11. The vase decorating the top tier is made in two halves, each from a golf ball-sized piece of paste rolled out to about 5mm (¼in) thick. Apply a thin smear of tin-slip or vegetable oil to the inside of the mould. Press the pastillage down into its contours, working it towards the edges. From time to time release it, and when it is evenly spread, trim any overlapping paste from the edges and leave to dry.

12. After about 24 hours it will be dry enough to handle with care. Use an emery board to smooth the edges, and join the halves together by piping a continuous line of icing along each edge. Pipe quite a thick line with a No. 2 or 3 nozzle, as the extra icing will help fill any gaps between the halves.

13. As in the case of the brackets mentioned earlier, royal icing again comes to the rescue in hiding any imperfections. An intricate pattern of parallel piped lines, swirls, scrolls or frills will cover up the flaws.

14. The vase can be extended by adding two circular frills to its top. To match the design of the vase with that of the cake, make handles for it, using the same technique as that described on p. 35.

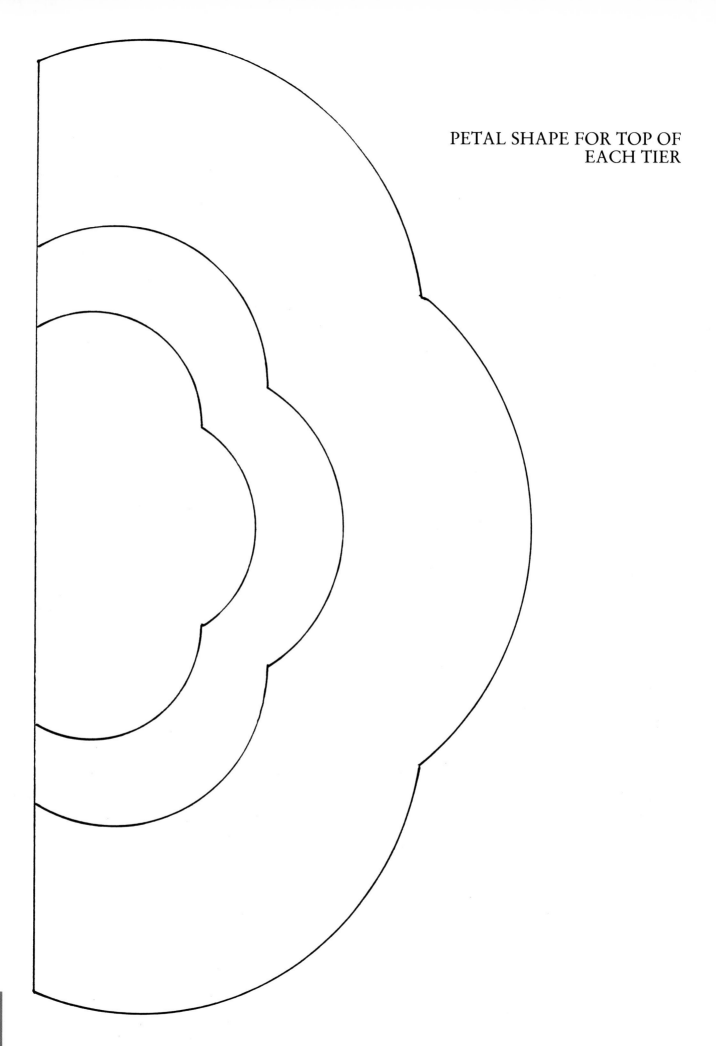

PETAL SHAPE FOR TOP OF
EACH TIER

DESIGN FOR SIDE OF CAKE

Basic outline

Finishing embellishments

SPRING TULIPS

Items needed to make this cake:

25cm (10in) teardrop-shaped cake
30cm (12in) teardrop-shaped cake
33cm (13in) acrylic teardrop cake board
38cm (15in) acrylic teardrop cake board
36cm (14in) white wedding cake box
41cm (16in) white wedding cake box
Dogbone modelling tool
Shell/knife modelling tool
Easy-flow icing smoother
No. 1 paint brush
2.5 metres 3mm willow green ribbon
Cornish cream concentrated paste food colour
Moss green concentrated paste food colour
Apple green concentrated paste food colour
Gum arabic glue
Large and small orchid throat cutters
Sheet of plastic or cardboard for templates
1.5kg (3lb) white almond marzipan
2kg (4lb) white sugarpaste
125g (4oz) Petal Paste

Here's a cake for a couple who would like a special cake with which to celebrate their wedding without it being too obviously a celebration wedding cake.

It may be based on a traditional fruit cake recipe, or it can be a madeira, genoese or any other variety of compact and firm sponge mix.

As illustrated, it is mounted on especially made transparent plastic cake boards, which in turn are positioned on a low, offset acrylic cakestand. This arrangement raises the smaller cake to a level of approximately 15cm (6in) above the table.

All the following cakes, with the exception of the Winter Wedding cake, are covered with sugarpaste (sometimes called rolled fondant or plastic icing) and the detailed instructions on using this medium follow.

COVERING WITH SUGARPASTE

Use the table below to estimate the quantity of sugarpaste you will need—approximately half the weight of the fruit cake.

15cm (6in) square or 18cm (7in) round—750g (1½lb)
20cm (8in) square or 23cm (9in) round—1kg (2lb)
25cm (10in) square or 28cm (11in) round—1.5kg (3lb)
30cm (12in) square or 32cm (13in) round—2kg (4lb)

These quantities can be varied slightly, but if too little is used, you will have difficulty covering the cake and forming the sugarpaste over the corners.

Measure the surface of the cake, up one side, across the top and down the other, using a rolling pin to give you an approximate measurement. Roll out the sugar paste on sifted icing sugar, making sure that it is prevented from sticking to the worktop by lifting and rotating it. Do not turn it over.

Before covering the cake with the sugarpaste, brush its marzipanned surface with just enough alcohol (rum, sherry or brandy) to make it tacky all over.

Lift the sugarpaste by draping it over a long rolling pin, and then lower it onto the cake. Remove the rolling pin. Use the heel of the palm of your hand to push it gently against the marzipan and to eliminate any air bubbles.

If the cake has corners, these must be attended to first. Flare the paste slightly to unfold any pleats and, using the palm of the hand, ease the sugarpaste onto the corner with an upward movement. If it cracks it can be repaired by gently smoothing it again using the heel of the palm. Repeat this process on the corners and then use the palm of the hand to press the sugarpaste against the sides of the cake.

Use a smoother or a palette knife to cut the excess material from around the base of the cake. It is important that there is no gap between the sugarpaste and the board.

Use a smoother to finish the sides by 'polishing' the sugarpaste with an even pressure. Be careful, but do not be too gentle. At this stage you can press the cake into shape quite successfully, as the sugarpaste is not yet hard. Use an 'ironing' action over the surface to eliminate any lumps or bumps. Once the cake is satisfactorily covered it can be placed onto its cake board.

INLAYING PATTERNS

There are several techniques for creating inlaid patterns and designs, but I have found that the method described here produces the neatest and also the quickest results, since it does not call for the accurate matching and interlocking of pieces of multicoloured icing.

The success of inlay work depends on the fact that the pieces of sugar to be inlaid are slightly firmer than the paste into which they are set. When making up the coloured paste for the pattern, use a mixture of half sugarpaste and half Petal Paste or pastillage. It is important to work quickly enough to cover the cake and apply the decoration in one session.

Before icing the cakes make your templates from cardboard or a piece of flexible acetate or similar plastic. Use the patterns shown on p. 46. Cover the cake with sugarpaste (see p. 40) and while the icing is still soft press the templates into position. Use a shell/knife modelling tool to indent their outline further into the icing surface. Then carefully remove the templates.

Roll the coloured paste so that it is just a little thicker than the depth of the impressed pattern. Lay the template on it and cut round it with a sharp craft knife. Remove the templates and moisten the indented area on the cake with gum arabic solution. Place the coloured icing into the impression and carefully press down so that the entire surface is once more even. Gentle smoothing will close any gaps between the coloured and white icing.

Once the leaves have been positioned and smoothed into place, the stems can be cut into strands using a knife or, if you have one, the 3mm Trenette attachment fitted to a pasta machine. The strands are then attached and smoothed into the surface of the cake.

These cakes have been placed on specially cut acrylic boards which are intended to be supported on a transparent two-tier acrylic cakestand. Conventional teardrop-shaped cake boards are available. An 8mm green ribbon has been stuck with piping gel around the bottom edge of the cake.

1. **Knead the sugarpaste to make it pliable, then roll it out on a non-stick workmat or a marble slab. Apply a light dusting of icing sugar to the worksurface to prevent the paste from sticking.**

4. **While the coating is soft, indent the pattern. You can make a template for this by cutting the shapes required from plastic or card which has roughly the stiffness of the shiny plastic used for shirt boxes. Use the original tracing as a reference to help position the patterns.**

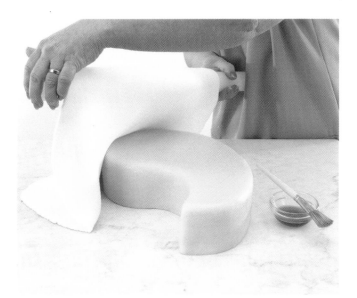

2. Moisten the surface of the marzipan by lightly brushing it with a little brandy or rum, then lift the paste on a rolling pin, and lay it carefully over the cake. Do this in one smooth, steady movement, as otherwise the icing may tear.

3. Use the open palms of your hands to smooth it into place. Try to avoid trapping air bubbles between the marzipan and the icing as you bring the two materials into contact with one another. Trim the edges with a palette knife and then use a handled smoother to polish the surface until it is smooth.

5. The indented areas are moistened with gum arabic solution before the cut out pastillage shapes are laid in place. It is helpful to cover the pieces which you are not ready to use with a piece of heavy plastic to stop them from drying prematurely. Special 'floppy mats' are available for this purpose.

6. When making thin strips of paste for the flower stems, the use of a pasta machine saves a lot of time. However, you can easily cut strips using a sharp kitchen knife and a ruler. Gum the back of each stem and then lay it carefully into position.

MAKING THE TULIPS

The pastillage tulips should be made well in advance of covering the cake as they need to be hard when they are pressed into the sugarpaste coating. Make a few extra ones in case you break any.

Make a very simple mould out of pastillage following the outline of the flower template shown here. The mould at its highest part should be about 1cm thick as this will give height to the finished bloom. Let this dry thoroughly before attempting to form the soft petals around it. Smear the mould with a little tin-slip or vegetable oil to stop the petals from sticking.

Use a cutter to make a pale yellow petal. Frill the scalloped edge and form it around the mould, cutting off any excess paste from the edges.

Cut an identical petal using darker-coloured paste, and divide it in half lengthwise. Take the left half and frill its scalloped edge. Moisten the pale yellow petal with gum arabic solution and position the half petal over it, with its straight edge following the outline of the right-hand side of the mould, and press the petal snugly into place.

Make the petal for the left-hand side of the tulip using the other piece of paste. Flare the frilled edges of the upper petals and allow to set.

To complete the design you will need five large and six small tulips.

7. **After all of the stems and leaves are positioned, the inner parts of the flowers are cut from very thinly rolled paste. Two flat petals are gummed together, and pressed into place on the cake, using a plastic icing smoother.**

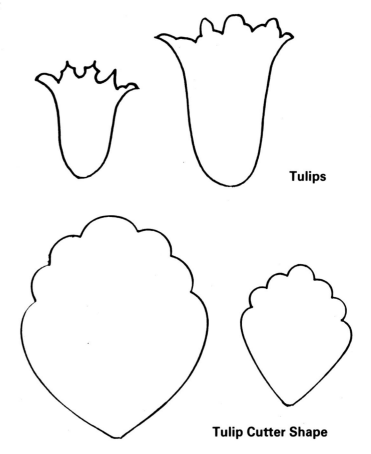

Tulips

Tulip Cutter Shape

44

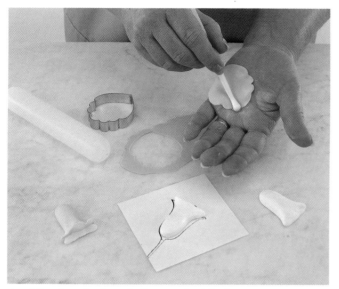

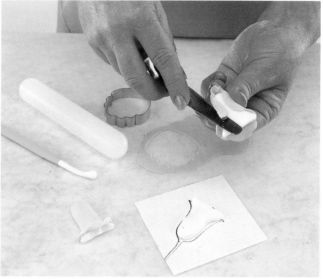

8. The head of each flower is dried over a mould, which is made from a piece of spare pastillage. The petals to be draped over the moulds are first frilled by holding them in the palm of the hand and gently pressing and rubbing the edges with a ball tool.

9. Trim off the excess paste so that the finished blooms will have neat edges when they are placed onto the cake. Extra time spent at this stage will reward you later on with a better finish to the cake's surface. Leave them to dry before attaching the outer petals.

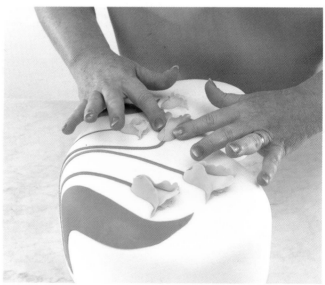

10. Cut one outer petal and then cut it in half. Frill the halves and stick them over the dried centre petal, using gum arabic solution to hold them in place. Use your fingers to mould them closely around the already hardened part of the flower. Be careful not to press too hard, or it may shatter.

11. While the coating is still soft, carefully mould against the lower edges of the outer petals, and then again smooth the icing around the flowers where it has been disturbed.

LEAF SHAPES

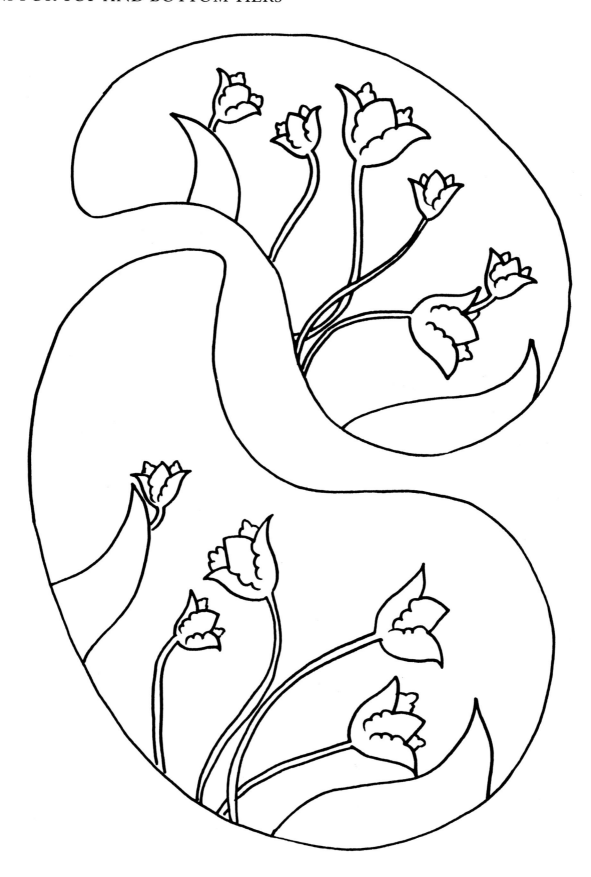

SUMMER LILIES

MEDIUM—needs some experience

Items needed to make this cake:

15cm (6in) square madeira cake
20cm (8in) square madeira cake
25cm (10in) square madeira cake
30cm (12in) square madeira cake
23cm (9in) square thin cake board + 25cm (10in) white wedding box
28cm (11in) square thin cake board + 30cm (12in) white wedding box
33cm (13in) square thin cake board + 36cm (14in) white wedding box
41cm (16in) square thin cake board + 41cm (16in) white wedding box
4 × 7.5cm (3in) white/pink spiral pillars
4 × 9cm (3.5in) white/pink spiral pillars
4 × 10cm (4in) white/pink spiral pillars
12 wooden food approved skewers
Writing nozzle No. 0
Shell nozzle No. 5
Parchment triangles
Garrett frill cutter
Baby face mould
Dogbone tool
Crimper No. 3
Crimper No. 31
Paint brush
Dusting brush
Piping gel
Small amount of brandy
Moss green concentrated paste food colour
Rose pink concentrated paste food colour
Apple green concentrated paste food colour
Cocktail sticks
750g (1½lb) buttercream for filling cakes
5kg (11lb) white almond marzipan
4kg (9lb) dark pink sugarpaste
2kg (4lb) pale pink sugarpaste
500g (1lb) Petal Paste
2 sugar-coated chocolate eggs—see pp. 52–4
3 sprays sugar flowers—see p. 56–61
Royal icing, dark pink, pale pink and green, for piping

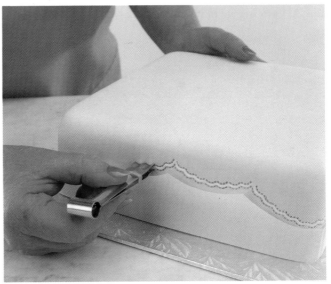

1. While the icing is still soft, cut a paper template to act as a guide for positioning the line of crimping around the sides of the cake. A rubber band over the crimper controls the extent to which its jaws will open, ensuring that each 'bite' into the icing is the same size.

2. Pipe a line of shells along the base of the cake using a No. 5 star nozzle. With its deeply incised teeth, the tip of this nozzle gives a strongly defined pattern which balances the prominent side decorations.

A four-tier cake is quite unusual although it is ideal for a large wedding with lots of guests. This is an informal cake, and its soft, rounded lines are characteristic of the sugarpaste style of icing which has become so popular in recent years.

With its frills and flounces and delicate pastillage flowers, it is a romantic offering for a happy occasion. The figures on the top tier—the bride and groom—have been made from sugar-coated chocolate eggs, and dressed in the same pastillage as used for the bouquets and frills, so there is a continuity of design from top to bottom.

Sometimes a tall cake can look overpowering, especially if, when set up on a banqueting table, it

towers above the seated guests. To minimise this effect I have used slightly different shades of pink icing to coat the cake, with the palest at the top and the deepest colour on the lowest tier.

An alternative to making a four-tier cake for a large wedding is to make just the three upper tiers for the complete cake, and to provide an extra cutting cake, which is iced but not decorated and taken straight to the kitchen. This provides a spectacular and photogenic cake with which to grace the table. It also saves time both in its decoration and, when the time comes, in cutting it into portions for the benefit of the guests at the reception.

3. The pattern to be embroidered (see p. 55), is applied when the coating has hardened. Scratch the details into the surface with a scriber so that you can see them clearly and pipe directly over the marks you have made using a No. 0 icing nozzle.

Cutter shape for frills and bride's dress

6. A fluted cutter shapes the circle of paste, while a second cutter removes the centre. The frilling is performed by rolling a cocktail stick around the edge. Press it down hard with the index finger and push it along by rotating it under the fingertip. The part just behind the stick will pucker into frills as the stick passes over it.

4. The embroidery at the corners is put on in the same way, gradually developing the details of the design. Do the outlines first before filling in the flowers and leaves. It is important to ensure that your icing is freshly beaten each time you use it. Well-beaten icing flows more freely.

5. To make the frills, use a small, very smooth rolling pin—a nylon or stainless steel one is best—to roll out the paste very thin. If the paste is too thick, when you try to frill the cocktail stick or frilling tool will simply cut it.

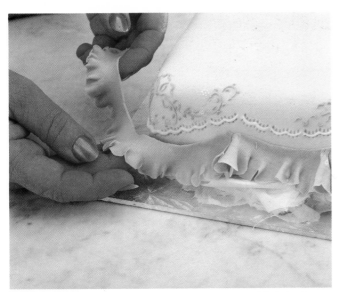

7. The first frill is attached about 5mm (¼in) below the crimped pattern. Make it from a mixture of pastillage and sugarpaste as this combination is strong enough to hold the frills up. Support them on lightly crushed tissues. Cocktail sticks may be used to hold out the frills if they are to be very prominent. To secure the frill, moisten the cake surface with a little water, and gently smooth it into place.

8. The second frill is set immediately below the crimped line after the lower one has set. It is eased into the crimping and smoothed off. Always position the lowest frill first, preferably letting it harden before adding further rows.

EGG FIGURES

Dress after rolling

Neck and wrist frills

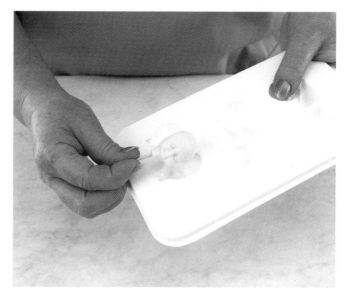

9. Smear a tiny amount of vegetable oil into the mould, then press a ball of skin coloured paste, about the size of a walnut, into it to form the features. The paste is rounded while it is still in the mould to form the shape of the entire head. Remove it immediately with a cocktail stick. When dry and with the features painted, royal icing 'hair' is piped and brushed on.

12. The morning coat is cut from two pieces of grey paste and joined at the back. The lapels are gently shaped before the coat is fitted onto the egg. The hat is made in three pieces, the crown, the brim and the cyclindrical body. The bride's dress must be frilled and crimped before draping in place over the underskirt.

10. The bodies are sugar-coated chocolate eggs. For the male figure, the egg is dusted with grey food colour, and put aside. The first stage of making the female figure is to stick the rounded end of the egg onto a 12.5cm (5in) square of sugarpaste which has been trimmed with a scallop crimper.

11. Roll out the pastillage, and use the templates on pp. 50, 52, and 54 to cut the garments. The foundation of the bride's gown is three sets of frills in different shades of pink. Each is formed using a fluted cutter, and the paste is elongated by rolling it in one direction only. A round portion towards the front of the oval is removed, and the frill is slipped over the upright egg onto which gum arabic solution has been painted to help the frill to stick.

13. The arms and sleeves for both figures are made as a single piece. The end of each arm is hollowed out to accommodate the wrists and hands which are formed from tiny cones. These are partially flattened, curved, and formed into fingers by snipping the paste with fine scissors. The small ball of paste in the background is all that is needed to make a hand.

14. Neither figure actually has legs! The groom is secured to the base by sticking the egg directly to the top of a pair of boots moulded from black sugarpaste. When both figures are in position, their inner arms are fixed in place, so that they are holding hands. The groom's top hat has been decorated with a pink hatband.

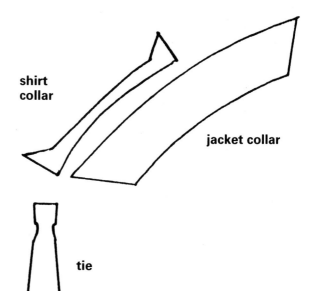

shirt collar

jacket collar

tie

15. The finished Bride and Groom are now ready to go on top of the cake.

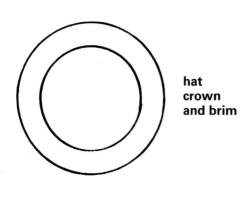

hat crown and brim

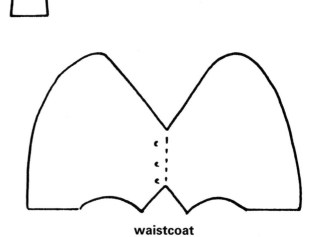

waistcoat

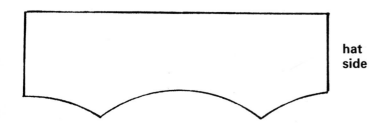

hat side

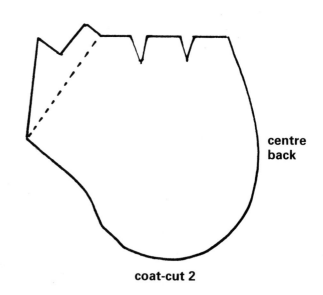

centre back

coat-cut 2

EMBROIDERY PATTERNS

SUGAR FLOWERS

The modelling of flowers has been practised for hundreds of years, although in the past they tended to be made of marzipan rather than pastillage. The following pages will give you, if you haven't already tried this fascinating side of sugarcraft, just a sample of what is possible in this area of cake decoration.

EQUIPMENT

A basic set of equipment for making sugar flowers must include a small nylon rolling pin, a 'dogbone' modelling tool and a ball tool for shaping and tooling the paste. It is helpful to have a selection of flower cutters. The most important for the beginner is a cutter set for making rose petals and leaves. Next is a single cutter for making carnations, and a set of three blossom cutters for filler flowers. It really doesn't matter whether they are made out of plastic or stainless steel so long as they are well shaped.

It is also important to obtain bundles of small white, yellow and pink stamens, some covered fine gauge floristry wire and a roll of green or white floristry tape. Dusting colour in pink, yellow and green is also required if the flowers are to have a realistic finish.

There are numerous other accessories important to the experienced cake decorator which are not included in the above list, and amongst the equipment which is very useful, but not absolutely vital, is a floppy mat used for preventing pastillage from drying prematurely, a resilient foam pad to mould flowers on, silicone rubber moulds for veining leaves, petals and flowers, and many more varieties of cutters, shades of stamens and gauges of floristry wire.

THE PARTS OF A FLOWER

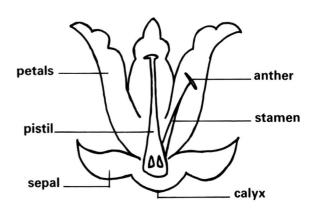

It is useful to know about the terms used in describing the individual parts of flowers. On the following pages you will come across them, as the method of making the flowers in the spray is explained.

ASSEMBLING A SPRAY

To make the three sprays of sugar flowers that are featured on this cake you will need approximately:

4 lilies
3 lily buds
30 sprays lily-of-the-valley
36 stephanotis
24 stephanotis buds
30 dark pink mexican-hat flowers
15 dark pink buds
36 light pink mexican-hat flowers
24 light pink buds
9 large ivy leaves
12 medium ivy leaves
12 small ivy leaves

To make the ivy leaves, use the cutters shown here and follow the instructions for leaves given with the Autumn cake.

LILIES

Equipment required:

Large lily cutters
Small funnel
Piece of dried corn husk
Pair of long tweezers
18swg green wire for bud
24swg green wire for pistil
33swg green wire for stamens
33swg white wire for petals
Light green floristry tape
Gum arabic solution

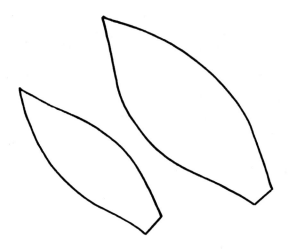

Lily petals

Lilies belong to a large group of plants that grow from bulbs. All of them bear extremely beautiful flowers in a wide range of colours. They have six large petals, six stamens and a large, gently curled pistil and stigma. When using lilies in bridal bouquets, florists always cut off the brown anthers found at the top of the stamens, as the pollen can stain fabric permanently. When making these flowers in sugar, take a little extra care, especially when painting and dusting the petals. The stamens are made by threading a small ball of paste onto a fine wire, which is then twisted between the fingers until the paste spreads down the wire and covers it. The pistil is at least ½in longer than the stamens and has a knob on the end which is divided into three and coloured brown.

Lily-of-the-valley

This is made using a small six-petal cutter. Roll out white flower paste so thin that you can read through it, and cut out the flowers. Place them on a foam pad and with a small modelling tool indent each of the six lobes, stroking them towards the centre of the flower to cup them. Pierce a hole at the centre and, when dry, insert a green stamen into the flower and fix in place with a tiny dab of icing.

Buds are made by rolling a small ball of paste onto the end of a gummed green stamen. Tape two or three buds and five or seven flowers to each piece of 28swg green wire.

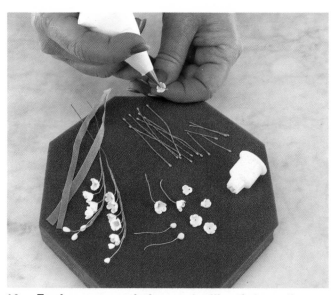

16.   Equipment needed to make lily-of-the-valley:

Lily-of-the-valley cutters
Pale green stamens
Light green floristry tape
28swg light green wire
Small amount of royal icing
Small ball tool
Foam sponge pad

Lily-of-the-valley

17. Make three ridged petals as shown on p. 67 and thread each onto a 33swg white wire. Press the face of the petal onto a piece of dried sweetcorn husk to give it texture. Use tweezers to raise the rib running down the back of each petal to greater prominence, then remove the petal and flare the edges with a ball tool. When all three wired petals have dried they must be dusted and painted and then taped around the stamens.

18. Three more petals, which are not wired, are made and painted, and while the paste is soft they are glued to the three wired ones. Six petals make up the completed flower, which must now be carefully arranged within a cone or a small funnel for support while the three soft petals dry out.

Mexican-hat flower

The sombrero has lent its name to a simple technique for making a variety of flowers. Every blossom begins with the same basic shape which is like a cone with its base flared out, and at this stage it has a similarity to a Mexican hat. The flower is cut, and threaded onto a wire with a tiny hook at its end. It is then placed into a little hole on a resilient foam pad, and a bundle of fine stamens is pushed into the centre while the paste is still soft. The impression of a calyx at the back of the flower is achieved by dusting it green. The steps involved in finishing basic flowers are shown in the foreground.

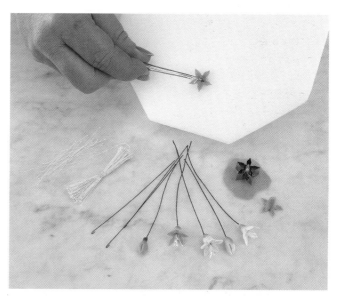

19. Equipment needed to make 'Mexican-hat flowers'

Jasmine cutter
Non-stick mini-rolling pin
28swg dark green wire
Pale pink stamens

Mexican-hat flower

Stephanotis

The same technique is used here in conjunction with a five-petalled cutter to make stephanotis. The petals are first pointed and slightly hollowed by drawing a blunt pointed rod over them. Then the back of the flower is elongated by rotating and gently squeezing it between the fingers. A hooked wire is inserted and a round centre hole formed with the pointed rod. This hole is then dusted yellow.

A bud is just a cylindrical piece of pastillage, pointed and indented at the tip with a pair of scissors, while the back is elongated like the mature flower.

A small star-shaped calyx is threaded over the wire to rest behind every flower, and secured with gum arabic solution.

20. Equipment needed to make stephanotis

Stephanotis cutter
Small star calyx cutter
26swg green wire

Stephanotis

Calyx cutter

WIRING A SPRAY

The diagram shows a skeleton of a posy with its seven individual branches leading towards a single thick stem. This may be bent up behind the spray, or placed in a small vase or plastic 'pick' which is designed specifically for inserting into the cake.

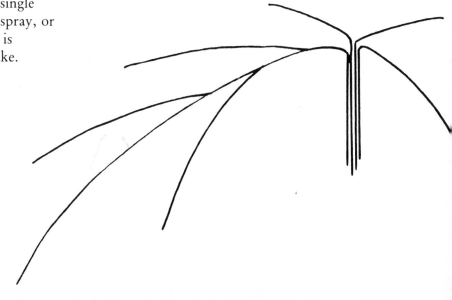

21. Tape together three or four small flowers and leaves, binding them with green self-adhesive floristry tape to form mini-sprays or 'branches' of the bouquet, one of which should be longer than any of the others.

22. As each spray is added, position it so that it is placed a little lower than its predecessors, so that the completed bouquet will be oval, not fan-shaped.

23. As the small sprays are joined on, their ends form the main stem. When viewed from behind, the placing of the later ones well below those bound together first can be clearly seen. Arrange them all facing outwards so that the back of the corsage is almost flat—as each spray is added it is taped either to the sides or above the main stem.

24. When the individual mini-sprays have been adjusted the finished lily and bud are carefully added and bound into place. This step is crucial in that the position of the specimen flower will influence the final arrangement of the rest of the spray. After adding the lilies, tape two more mini-sprays to the main stem.

Items needed to make this cake:

15cm (6in) hexagonal cake
20cm (8in) hexagonal cake
25cm (10in) hexagonal cake
20cm (8in) hexagonal cake board and 20cm (8in)
    white wedding box
25cm (10in) hexagonal cake board and 25cm (10in)
    white wedding box
36cm (14in) hexagonal cake board and 36cm (14in)
    white wedding box
Scriber
Fine paint brushes
Selection of petal dusts
Dark brown concentrated food colour
3 metres willow green 3mm wide ribbon
2kg (4lb) white almond marzipan
4kg (8lb) ivory-coloured sugarpaste (1.5kg (3lb) is
    used for covered boards)
500g (1lb) Petal Paste for leaves, etc.

A wedding timed to take place in late summer or autumn, when the days are still long and the weather warm, has obvious advantages over a spring wedding. It is also an ideal time for the creative cake decorator to translate the symbols of nature's bounty into a theme for a seasonal wedding cake.

The three-tier hexagonal cake covered in ivory-coloured sugarpaste (as described on p. 40) and decorated in autumnal colours, in delicate hues of red, russet and brown, demonstrates the techniques of drawing and painting in icing, and of pastillage floristry, and combines them on a tiered cake of simple elegance.

For all its distinction and style, it needs a minimum of piping in royal icing; a fact which may be seen as an advantage by cake decorators for whom time is at a premium. The berries and leaves can be made in spare moments while watching television, and if you interleave them between layers of tissue paper or kitchen roll, and store them in a cardboard box, it is unlikely that they will come to harm.

Most varieties of leaf are made using the technique illustrated, and so long as you make a note of the physical shape and colouration of the particular foliage you wish to reproduce, the description given here has a wide general application.

1. A mask of greaseproof paper is used to prevent the dusting colour from falling in the wrong place. The part closest to the horizon is relatively faint compared with the foreground, where more layers of dusting colour are allowed to build up. See p. 72 for outline patterns for the hills.

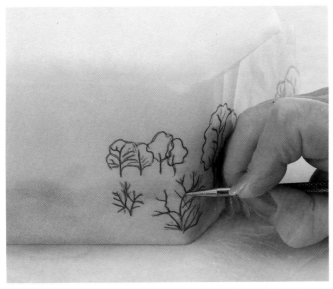

2. The silhouettes of trees and the foreground details are added with the help of a tracing on greaseproof paper as a guide. Use a scriber to scratch the outline through the greaseproof onto the surface of the icing.

3. Ordinary paste food colour is used to paint the tree trunks and details of the twigs and branches. A final coating of orange, yellow and red dusting colour is stippled onto the trees to establish the soft, autumn shading of the leaves.

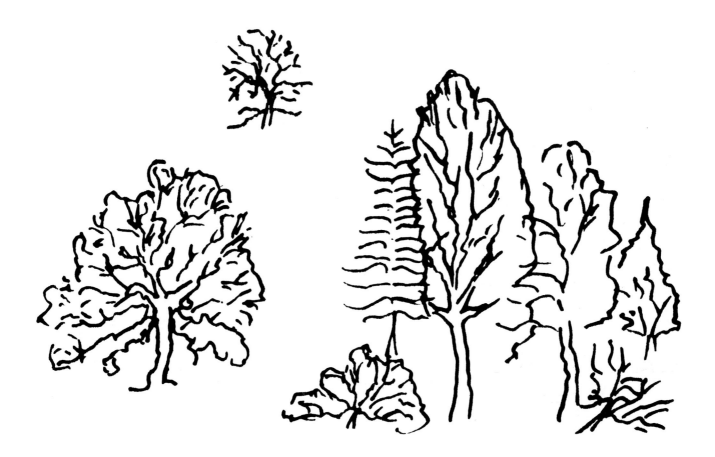

LEAF SEQUENCE
FOR AUTUMN CAKE

Equipment needed to make spray of autumn leaves:

Set maple leaf cutters
Set ivy leaf embossers
Set oak leaf cutters
Set oak leaf veiners
Set rose leaf cutters
Set rose leaf veiners
Set chrysanthemum leaf cutters
Set blossom plunger cutters
Selection of floristry wire in various gauges from 18
   to 33swg
Selection of different-coloured floristry tapes
Selection of dusting colours
Selection of paste food colours
Confectioner's glaze
Mini-rolling pins
Needle point modelling tool
Gum arabic solution
Pastillage floppy mat
Petal Paste in various colours

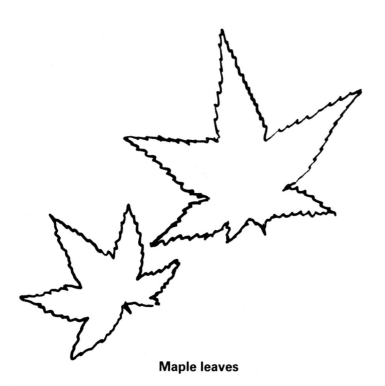

Maple leaves

4.   Colour the pastillage and roll it into a strip, which is left fairly thick to form a ridge along an imaginary centre line. It's easy if you have two small mini-rolling pins which are laid parallel to one another along the centre line. Press them down and roll them away from one another to thin the paste right to its edges.

7.   Carefully insert the stalk and then squeeze the paste between two silicone rubber veining moulds to give it an authentic leaf-like texture. The moulds are casts taken from natural leaves, so they reproduce every marking and vein.

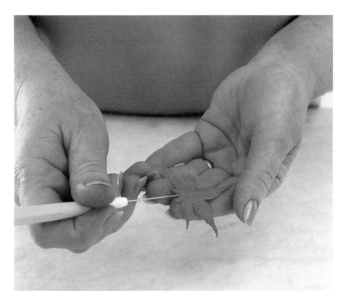

5. The ridge will form the central line on the back of each leaf. It's the rib from which all the veins radiate. If you have sufficient paste to make two leaves at once, flatten a small area of the rib at the points where the leaf tips will be, and align your cutter along the centreline of the paste.

6. Cut it out, and pierce a hole into the thickened section of the leaf to make room for a stalk made from 30swg florist's wire. Use covered wire, and if necessary use the same food colour as used for the leaves to paint it to match, by drawing the wire over a piece of colour-impregnated sponge.

8. While the leaf is still soft and pliable, lay it on a piece of kitchen roll, and dust it with suitable autumnal shades of colour, then turn it over and dust the back. For really authentic colours, pick up a few leaves and try to match them. You will be surprised at how brightly coloured they are.

9. Dip the leaf into confectioner's glaze diluted with 10 per cent alcohol and hang it from a rack to dry. The glaze seals the colour, and imparts a slight shine. After five minutes the paste is nearly dry, and at this stage is still flexible so that you can bend the leaves to curl them into natural shapes. To obtain a high shine, repeat the dipping and drying several times.

Oak leaves

Rose leaves

10. Autumn leaves demonstrate the ravages of their exposure to wind and rain with dark-edged holes, spots and tears. You can imitate nature by burning holes in them with a red-hot needle, or by singeing them in a smoky candle flame. Dark spots of colour can also be added by flicking powder colour onto the freshly glazed leaves.

13. A rose hip is made from a cone of cream flower paste which is threaded onto a hook of 24swg wire. When set, it is coloured with yellow dust on one side. The red paste colour is used directly from the jar using a piece of foam sponge. It is then coated with red dusting colour, and sealed by dipping it into confectioner's glaze twice to impart a high shine.

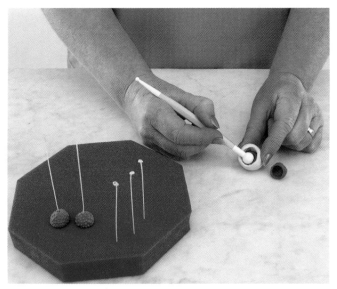

11. Acorns are made in two parts, the nut and its cup. Make a mould for the cup by pressing a natural acorn cup into modelling clay and letting it dry. Pastillage cups are then made by pressing some paste into the mould with a ball tool, removing it, and hollowing the inside, so that it will comfortably house the acorn. Insert a hooked 26swg wire into the base and leave to dry.

12. The inside of the cup is painted with gum arabic solution, and the nut is inserted. Note that each smooth hand-made nut has a small point on its tip. Only the acorns, not the cups, are glazed. Oak leaves are made in the same way as the maple leaves described earlier, except that the edges are tooled with a ball tool to give them their distinctive corrugated appearance.

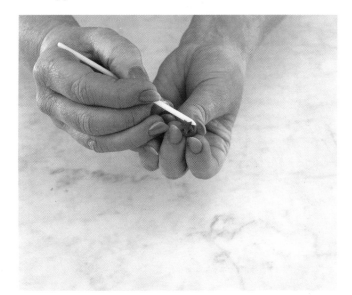

14. The calyx on the tip of the rosehip can be as large as the seed pod itself, although in this case it is just brown flower paste shaped with a miniature calyx cutter. The star is moulded on a resilient foam pad and secured with gum arabic solution to the tip of the rose hip.

15. The calyx of hawthorn berries is made by snipping the top part with pointed scissors. Make five small incisions around the end of the berry, and lift the cut portions into a crown shape. The shoulder below the crown should be accentuated by enlarging it with a cocktail or modelling stick. Pull the berry onto a fine wire, paint the calyx dark brown, and glaze the entire berry.

Hawthorn leaves

16. They are assembled into clusters of up to ten, by wiring them onto 28swg wire, and binding them with olive green floristry tape. Build up the woody stem to which the cluster is attached by winding extra tape over it. To make it appear gnarled, scratch the surface and roughen it with a sharp scriber, then paint it with dark brown colour.

Hop leaf and flowers

19. Wire the arrangement in two halves, oak and rose in one half, maple and hawthorn in the other, and fix the hops to the centre once the halves are joined. Use extra thick 18swg wire to strengthen the spray as it becomes bigger. Because heavy gauge wire is very stiff use a pair of electrical pliers to bend it.

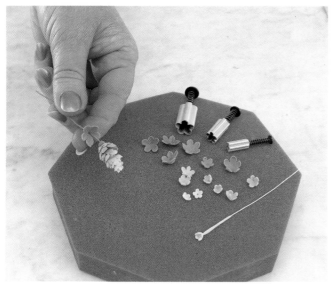

17. Colour three small pieces of pastillage cream, parchment, and a very pale dull green. Use blossom cutters to make a dozen hop flowers in graduated sizes and colours. Roll a piece of paste onto the end of a wire and thread the blossom flowers over it, starting with the smallest. Make the last three blossoms from slightly thicker paste, so that they can be enlarged by stretching their petals with a ball tool, before they are threaded onto the wire.

18. When dry, dust with cream colour at the tip, graduating to moss green at the base. Leaves, flowers and berries are then taped into small sprays. Start at the tip with the smallest pieces and add larger items as you work towards the base of the spray. Wrap a 10cm (4in) piece of floristry tape around the end of a piece of 33swg wire and curl this round a pencil to form the tendril for the hop flowers.

20. The large arrangement which is now assembled from a collection of individual pieces representing maple, hawthorn, hops, roses and oak leaves is just rested on top of the cake.

21. This spray of autumnal nuts, berries, and leaves is a colourful alternative to a decoration of flowers. If you wish to make an autumn spray using other varieties, use material which does not grow too large in real life.

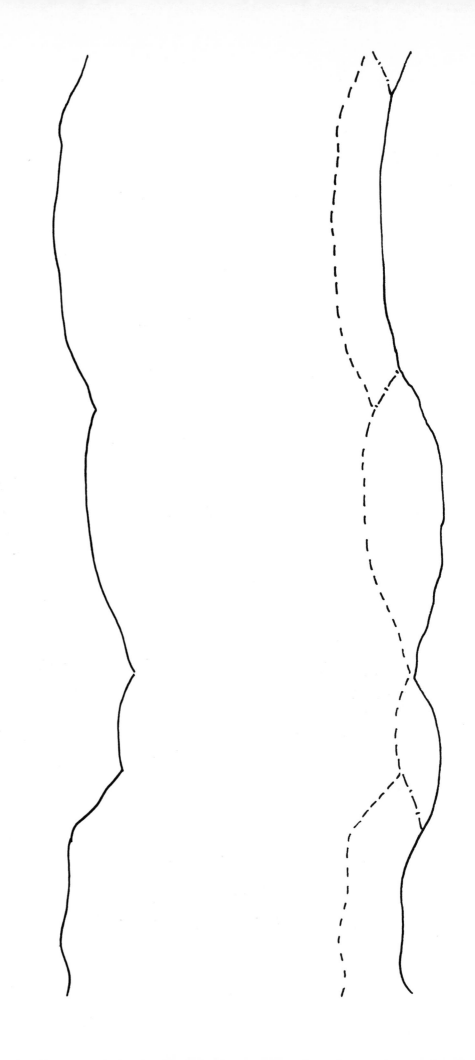

OUTLINE PATTERNS
FOR HILLS

OUTLINE PATTERNS
FOR TREES

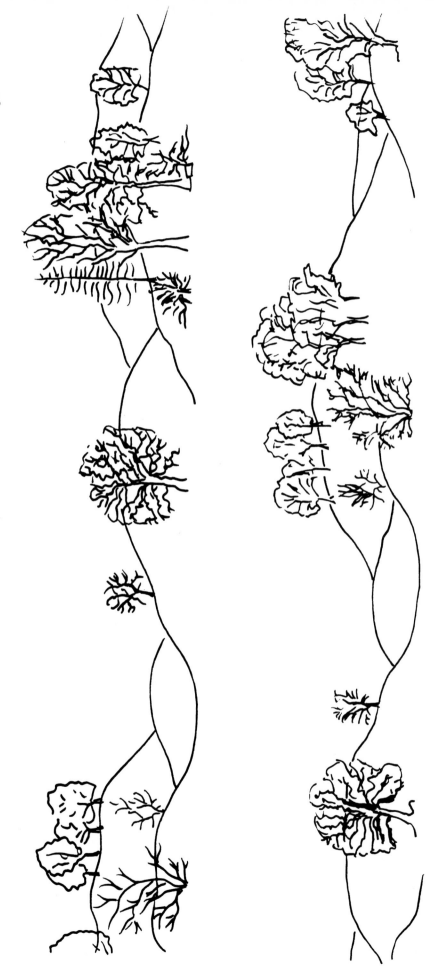

Items needed to make this cake:

15cm (6in) round sponge cake 7.5cm (3in) high
20cm (8in) round sponge cake 7.5cm (3in) high
25cm (10in) round sponge cake 5cm (2in) high
36cm (14in) round sponge cake 7.5cm (3in) high
20cm (8in) round thin cake card
25cm (10in) round thin cake card
20cm (8in) round thin cake card plus 20cm (8in)
   white wedding box
41cm (16in) round thick cake board
46cm (18in) round thick cake board plus 46cm (18in)
   white wedding box
12 wooden food-approved skewers
3kg (6lbs) American frosting (5 times the recipe
   given on p. 93) *(this is enough to layer the sponge
   cakes as well as coat them)*
1.5 metres pleated ribbon for base board
6 metres 3mm ribbon for sprays
1 metre fine nylon tulle 15cm (6in) wide cut into
   7.5cm (3in) lengths and gathered and wired into
   sprays
4 sprays commercial white holly berries or similar
   decoration
Glass church or cake top decoration

The problem with some cake decoration books is
that although written with the best of intentions to
satisfy a wide spectrum of readers, they end up by
becoming books by cake decorating enthusiasts for
other cake decorating enthusiasts.

Since it is my intention to avoid this pitfall, I have
made a basic buttercream decorated sponge cake in a
manner which is sometimes described as 'American
Frosting'. It is very sweet compared with a royal
iced fruit cake, very easy to make and, above all, it is
very quick. Unlike the other cakes featured in this
book it requires no specialised tools. So long as you
can find a knife with which to spread the frosting
you will have all the equipment you need.

The cakes will need to be made during the week of
the wedding, and each tier, apart from the 15cm
(6in), is made up of layers frosted together. The
cake layers can be baked well in advance, cooled,
then wrapped in a plastic bag and foil and frozen.
Unwrap and thaw at room temperature for three to
four hours before you start decorating them.

The long plastic pillars supporting the upper tier
can be purchased or hired from cake decoration
shops. The glass church decorating the top was
commissioned from a local craftsman whose

1. **Whether or not the cake is marzipanned, it is
   important to provide extra support for the layers
   going on top of it. Use food-approved wooden
   skewers cut to the exact height of the cake.
   Push them down through the cake so that the
   tops are flush with the surface.**

2. **The individual cakes, just before they are iced,
   are shown here to illustrate the method of
   assembly. Each layer is placed on a board of the
   same diameter, and each layer is skewered, so
   that it supports the one above it. You can just
   see the edges of the boards beneath the three
   upper layers. In practice the pillars and top tier
   do not go into place until after all the layers are
   iced.**

mainstream activity is restoring windows in real churches!

Many brides who would like to make and decorate their own cake wish that they had time to learn the formal skills of sugarcraft. With so many other pressures to meet organisational deadlines in the weeks leading up to the wedding day, this desire is difficult to fulfil, but there are ways around the problem. The Winter Wedding shows that a lovely cake, decorated in about two hours, can be as attractive as those requiring considerably more time. Some planning is obviously required, since you will have to shop around for a suitable top ornament, and for appropriate ribbons and other ready-made decorations to set on the tiers.

In this case the church was made in advance from several small pieces of 2mm-thick glass, and the ribbons and tulle were then carefully selected to echo the natural colour showing through the edges of the glass. This colour scheme was followed throughout, even to the extent of wrapping coloured ribbon round wooden skewers and inserting them into the hollow centres of the three clear plastic pillars that support the upper tier.

Ruffles similar to those surrounding the base of the cake are available by the yard from some cake decoration shops, but if it is impossible to find anything suitable they may be made from wide ribbon which is merely pleated and stapled onto the cake's base board. When the cake board bearing the lower tier is laid in position it covers the inner edge of the ruffles and adds a final touch of excitement to the design. Ribbon of the same colour can also be used to trim the sides of the cake boards. It can be secured with the sort of paste glue used for sticking paper.

The frosting was left white, but it may be tinted in a pastel shade by beating a small amount of paste food colour into the mixture. The addition of a few drops of flavouring such as vanilla essence or peppermint can add to the flavour of the frosting, and will take the edge off its sweetness.

3. **Although they don't have to be marzipanned, it makes them easier to coat with frosting. They are frosted individually before they are stacked. The frosting is laid on the cake and patted into place with a knife blade. Do the sides, and then assemble the layers.**

6. **The cake is finished by decorating it with ribbon loops. A length of ribbon approximately 40cm (15in) long is twisted into three loose loops around the finger, and a short length of ribbon is laid beneath it. A small piece of floristry wire is used to bind the arrangement together.**

4. Frost the remaining parts of the lower three cakes and the top of the upper tier. The more vigorous the action of patting, the more prominent will be the peaks on the icing.

5. Edible glitter can be scattered over the cake to add sparkle to the rough iced surface. The glitter is very easy to make as it is just gum arabic solution left to evaporate on a non-stick surface. When it is dry the residue is scraped up, and it is ready to use.

7. Ribbon loops, small gathered rectangles of tulle and white artificial Christmas berries and leaves are combined into a spray bound with white florist's tape. Make three or four of these and arrange them on the cake.

8. The glass church is 'snowed' with frosting to complete the winter scene. An alternative cake top decoration could be a glass vase, filled with small cream or white silk flowers, or a traditional bride and groom ornament.

CHOCOHOLIC'S DREAM

MEDIUM—some experience required

Items needed to make this cake:

20cm (8in) vanilla madeira cake
20cm (8in) chocolate cake
30cm (12in) vanilla madeira cake
30cm (12in) chocolate cake
20cm (8in) round thin cake card
30cm (12in) round thin cake card
30cm (12in) round gold cake board and 30cm (12in)
  white wedding box
38cm (15in) round gold cake board and 41cm (16in)
  white wedding box
Sieve
Wire rack
Tray for catching chocolate
Ball tool
Garrett frill cutter
Rose leaf cutter
Rose leaf veiner
Firm sponge pad
Paint brush
1.25kg (2lb 8oz) superior dark 'chocolate' coating
2.5kg (5lb) white almond marzipan
250g (8oz) white 'chocolate' coating
125g (4oz) piping gel
4 × 140g liquid glucose
Gold food colour

1.   **Alternative assembly for cakes—this photo
     shows how the cake can be set up on a low
     acrylic stand.**

You don't have to ice a cake with icing at all. This is
the fulfilment of a chocoholic's dream—the coating
and all the decoration is made with real chocolate,
and when it is cut you will see that the cake itself is a
chequerboard of chocolate and vanilla sponge which
has been brushed with chocolate liqueur to give it
that extra zing!

If you achieve a good coating which properly seals
the cake from the air, the sponge will stay fresh for
up to a week. You will also have to take into account
the fact that your guests will expect to receive a
larger slice of sponge than of fruit cake, so it is more
likely that every morsel of this will be consumed at
the wedding reception, and you may have to provide
an extra 'cutting' cake to cater adequately for
everyone.

If you bake two of each size sponge, this will
produce two finished cakes, one of which can be
covered with chocolate but not decorated, and left in
the kitchen for cutting into all those extra slices.

Put the chocolate in a bowl over a saucepan of hot
water (not boiling) and make sure that the water
does not come into contact with the bowl, as this

2.   **When the chequerboard is cut it reveals this
     fascinating pattern. It is the cookery equivalent
     of tins of striped paint!**

may cause it to get too hot. Gently stir it until all the chocolate has melted.

You can melt chocolate in the microwave in 4–5 minutes (milk or white chocolate will need slightly less time), but make sure you have it on low (defrost) setting and stir it frequently.

For a 20cm (8in) cake, melt about 500g (1lb), as although you will only use about three-quarters of this on the cake, you must have enough to cover the cake all in one pouring. It is better to have too much than not enough!

Use a sharp warmed knife to release the cake from the wire tray and then position it on a cake board, using a little chocolate to stick it in place. Pipe around the edge of the cake with a No. 8 star nozzle, using chocolate which has been thickened with a few drops of glycerine.

3. **The chequerboard effect is made by cutting concentric rings of sponge from chocolate and madeira sponge mixes, and then mixing and reassembling the pieces to create contrasting colours.**

6. **The marzipan coating provides a firm and even surface for the final luxurious cover of real chocolate. Gently warm the dark chocolate in a double saucepan and, when melted, pour it through a sieve straight on to the cake.**

4. Three sets of rings are layered together, and joined with a spread of chocolate flavoured buttercream. The cakes can be brushed with chocolate liqueur to give them added flavour—do this before starting to spread the buttercream.

5. The whole cake is sealed under a thin layer of buttercream to prevent any loose crumbs of cake from falling away. Then the cake is chilled in a refrigerator to harden it in preparation for the next stage.

7. The sieve helps to regulate the flow of chocolate, making it much easier to achieve an even coating. Do not allow the chocolate to overheat, or it will develop an unattractive white 'bloom' when it cools.

8. Notice that the cake is rested on a wire rack inside a tray, so that any excess chocolate can be recovered for future use. Once the whole cake is covered, tap the tray up and down—this disperses the chocolate evenly and will burst any air bubbles. Leave the cake for a few minutes for the chocolate to set.

CHOCOLATE LEATHER

To make this you will need:

155g (5oz) liquid glucose
185g (6oz) melted chocolate

9. Liquid glucose, warmed in boiling water to make it flow more easily, is mixed with melted chocolate. It is possible to use milk, plain or white chocolate for making this moulding chocolate or 'leather'.

CHOCOLATE FRILLS

12. To create depth in the frill, work it with a ball tool. Do this by gently rotating the ball tool in each of the scallops. In doing so, you stretch the chocolate leather, causing it to pucker into gentle corrugations.

10. Stir the mixture until it thickens. This process only takes a few seconds, so be ready to tip it onto a work surface in preparation for the next stage.

11. Knead it as it cools. It will quickly take on a glossy appearance and develop a rubbery texture. Leave the mixture to cool for at least two hours. It does not have to be used all at once, and can be stored almost indefinitely in an airtight box in the fridge.

13. Gold non-toxic paint is widely used by cake decorators for highlights and contrasts. It is painted onto the chocolate, and as it contains very sticky varnish, make sure that you wash out the brush immediately after you have finished. Unless you are using pure gold leaf it is advisable to remove the gold-painted pieces before consuming the cake.

14. After the gilding is dry, the frill is opened up and attached to the cake by pressing it gently onto a line of piping gel which has been painted onto the chocolate coating. Indent the top edge of the frill with the small end of the ball tool for a decorative finish.

WHITE CHOCOLATE ROSES

The large chocolate roses are made from white chocolate leather although a similar technique could be used to make them from sugarpaste or even marzipan. As the petals are densely packed, only the visible edges need to appear thin; the other edges around the petals can be left quite thick.

Begin by rolling a ball of chocolate, and mould it into a cone about 5cm (2in) high. Place this on a worktop. Next take a pea-sized ball of paste and put it into the top of a polythene bag, then squash the ball and work the edges with a fingertip until they are as thin as possible. Remove the petal from the bag by peeling the plastic away from the chocolate. Wrap it round the cone with the top of the petal about 5mm (¼in) above the tip of the cone. Squeeze the lower edge of the petal against the cone, and slowly form a waist right round the cone at this level. Ensure that the top of the petal, where it protrudes above the tip of the cone, is completely closed into a tight spiral shape.

Take a second pea-sized ball of chocolate leather and thin it the same way. The centre of this one is placed over the point where the first petal overlaps itself, but slightly higher on the cone. Stick the left edge to the cone by squeezing it gently, but leave the right edge temporarily free. Gently curl the top edge outwards.

The third, fourth and all subsequent petals are made in the same way as the first, and are tucked under the open side of the one previously attached, which should then be squeezed into place. In this way the petals are made to overlap one another. The amount of overlap should be about half the width of each petal. As the rose grows in size the petals should be made slightly larger, and stretched slightly as they are secured to the cone. The upper edge of each one should be gently rolled outwards, away from the centre of the rose, to create the natural look of a mature, opened flower.

When the rose is large enough, squeeze the lower part of the cone to waist it again and to consolidate all the petals, then release the flower from the cone at this point with a horizontal cut.

15. **A cone of white chocolate leather is shaped by hand, and its base is indented with many tiny impressions using the small ball tool to represent stamens deep down inside the flower. This base eventually becomes the centre of an open rose.**

18. **Rosebuds have a prominent calyx, which gradually folds back as the flower opens. With white rosebuds, use dark chocolate for contrast. Rose leaves (made with a rose leaf cutter) can be gilded, or simply made in white chocolate or dark chocolate and left undecorated.**

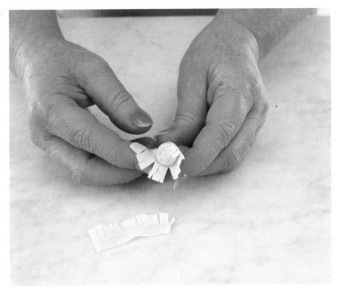

16. A narrow strip is rolled out very thinly, and then fringed along one of its sides. Snip the fringe with scissors, or use a knife to cut it. This strip is then rolled tightly around the base of the cone. The fringed ends will come to represent the stamens in the flower, so make sure that they are standing up above the top of the cone.

17. When the first row of five overlapping petals (each petal smaller than a pea) has been arranged around the fringe, a further row of slightly larger ones is added. Continue to add extra petals, gently bending the edges of the outer ones away from the centre of the flower.

19. When all the flowers and leaves have been made and set, assemble them on the cake, starting with the roses on the cake board and working up the side of the cake. The completed flowers are secured to the cake with a little melted chocolate. You have to work quickly or the chocolate will set in your piping bag.

20. Roses and buds of differing sizes, when used in conjunction with gilded leaves and frills, make an unusual and eye-catching cake decoration.

CLOUD NINE CAKE

MEDIUM—some experience required

For this cake you will need:

41cm (16in) × 25cm (10in) oval fruit cake
53cm (21in) × 35cm (13½in) oval board
  (*cut by hand from chipboard and covered with
  silver cake paper*)
No. 32 scallop crimper without teeth
1.75kg (3½lb) white almond marzipan
2.5kg (5lb) white sugarpaste
2kg (4lb) Petal Paste
Blue, pink, lavender dusting colours
Blue and pink airbrushing colours
Dusting brush
Royal icing, small amount for piping

If you would like to escape from the traditional
symbolism of the formal wedding cake, why not try
something like this? The idea came to me while I was
browsing through an oriental book on theatre
design. Pastillage is a versatile product, and although
most cake decorators think of it only as the preferred
medium for making delicate sugar flowers, it has
long been used by confectioners for sculpting large
classical designs with pillars, plinths and pedestals,
for baskets and cornucopias overflowing with exotic
fruit, and for figurines and animals. When rolled out
to a thickness of about three millimetres, it is ideal
for making the kind of flowing shapes illustrated
here.

The background, the dancing images of the bride
and groom, and the clouds forming the frieze, are all
made from the same pastillage, which in these
examples has been given more strength than the
flower maker's version of gumpaste, by the addition
of an extra ten per cent by weight of gum tragacanth.

Each pattern should be trimmed when it is dry.
The irregular and untidy edges can be smoothed by
rubbing them carefully on a small pad of two
hundred grit glasspaper or manicurist's emery
board.

All the clouds and the backdrop have been made
from plain white pastillage, and highlights have been
created with a light misting of colour, applied
through an inexpensive aerosol-powered airbrush.

The shadows beneath the dancing couple, which
heighten the dramatic effect, were created by
stippling some colour onto the surface through a
stencil.

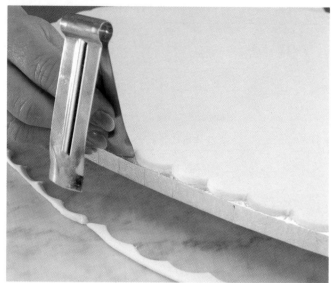

1. **Cutting a scallop pattern into the icing covering
    the cake board gives an interesting finish to the
    edge of the cake board. A large plain scalloped
    crimper is the ideal tool for this purpose. Just
    press one of the ends into the sugarpaste to cut
    the scallop, and remove any unwanted material.**

2. **The cloud effect is airbrushed through a paper
    stencil from which a series of crescents have
    been cut. They have been 'feathered' to soften
    the edges of the sprayed areas. When spraying
    hold the nozzle about 15cm (6in) away from the
    stencil. A pattern for the airbrushing is given on
    p. 91.**

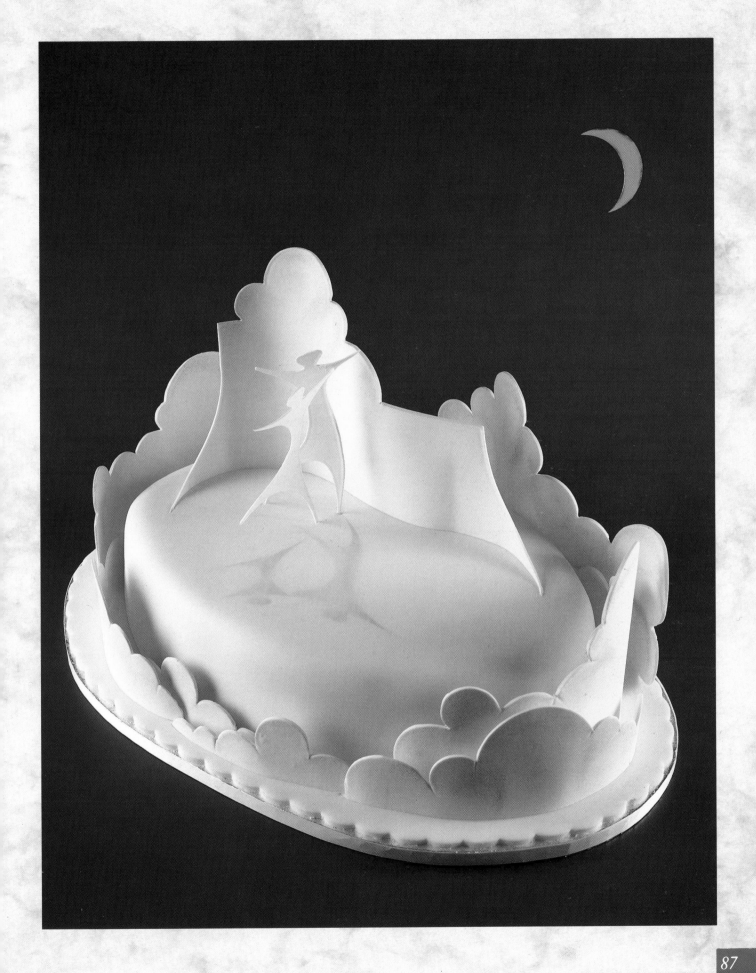

In order to obtain the effect of 'floating' on air, it is necessary to adjust the position of the figures very carefully. Because the design is so slender, it is advisable to support the figures with pieces of foam sponge if transporting the cake.

There are no wires or supports in any of the sugar pieces, so they must be placed into the soft sugarpaste of a freshly covered cake (see p. 40 for how to cover a cake with sugarpaste). Planning is essential. The pastillage pieces must be hard before the cake is covered.

Plan of cake

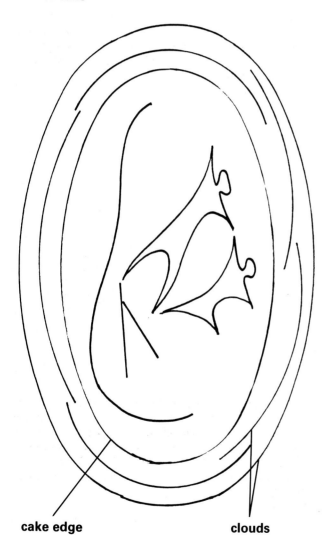

cake edge   clouds

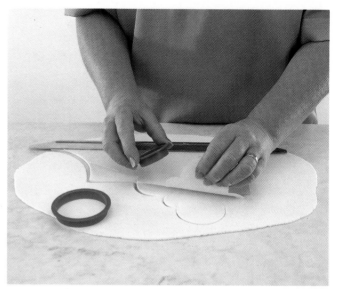

3. The pastillage, which should be rolled to a thickness of about 3.5mm (⅛in), is cut using a sharp knife and several different-sized circular biscuit cutters. A paper template will be helpful in achieving the correct shape (see p. 91).

6. The shadows of the dancing pastillage figures are applied to the top of the cake. The icing is still soft at this stage, so work carefully. Cut a stencil from the pattern on p. 90 and lay it on the cake, then gently stipple the colour. It is best to use dusting colours mixed with cornflour to dilute their strength. Two shades are used and gently blended on the cake—pink and blue.

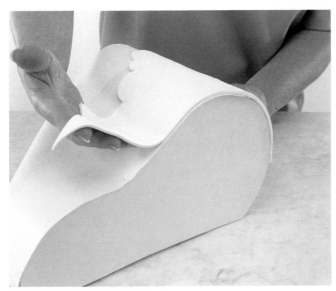

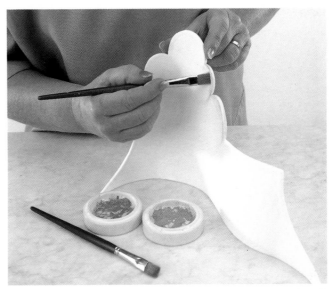

4. The paste is draped over a former so that it will harden into the correct profile. It is important to let it dry on a flexible surface such as that of a non-stick silicone rubber workmat, which will follow the exact contours of the polystyrene mould.

5. It takes about 24 hours for the paste to dry hard enough for the next stage, which is to apply the delicately tinted pattern. If you don't wish to use an airbrush, you can stipple dusting colour onto the pastillage.

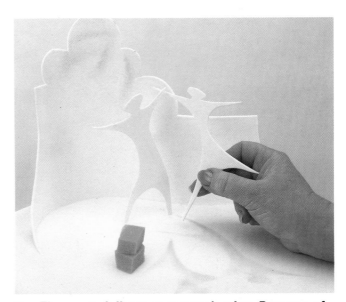

7. The large pastillage off-pieces are pressed into the sugarpaste to indent their positions. A thick line of royal icing is piped into these areas, and the pieces are pressed carefully into place. If any icing is squeezed out, clean it off with a soft damp brush.

8. The most delicate part now begins. Because of their fragility the dancing figures must be made from extra strong pastillage so that they can be pressed directly into the cake. Adjust them so that they are just touching, and until the sugarpaste has hardened, support them with a pad of soft foam sponge.

figure cut-outs

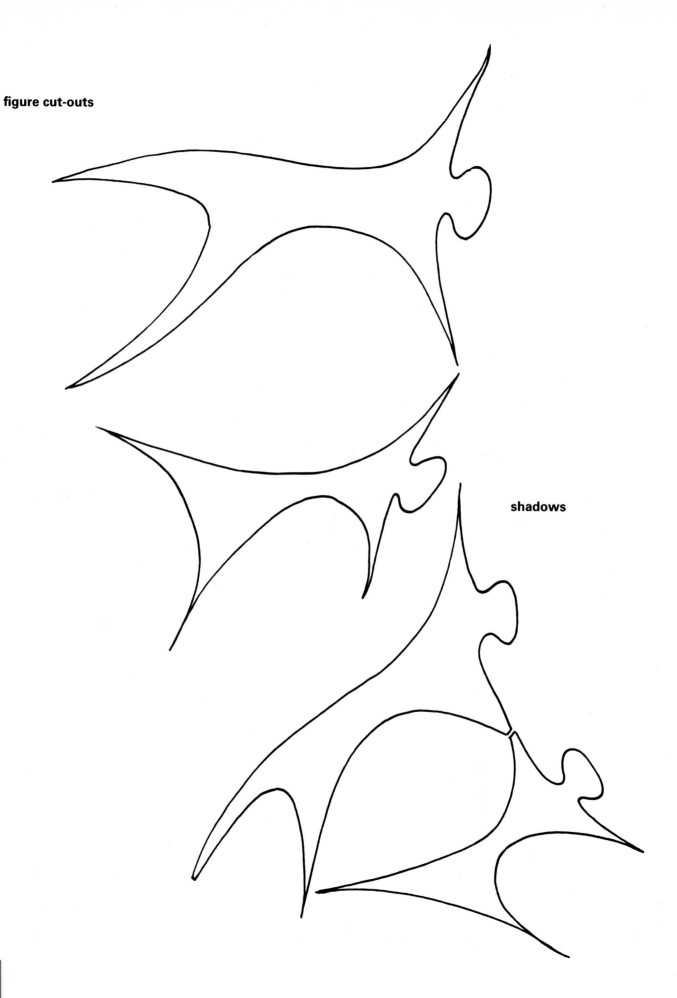

shadows

cloud on cake

airbrushing guide

side clouds

91

CAKE AND ICING RECIPES

RICH FRUIT CAKE

250g (8oz) sultanas
250g (8oz) currants
250g (8oz) raisins
125g (4oz) glacé cherries
50g (2oz) ground almonds
½ cup (4fl oz) brandy, sherry or orange juice
250g (8oz) plain flour
60g (2oz) self-raising flour
1 tsp each mixed spice and cinnamon
¼ tsp nutmeg
Pinch of salt
250g (8oz) butter
250g (8oz) dark brown sugar
4 eggs (lightly beaten)

Pre-soak the fruit overnight in the alcohol or orange juice. Mix the flours, spices and almonds. Beat together the butter and sugar and add the eggs a little at a time. Stir in the flour and fruit alternately in small quantities. Do not beat. Turn mixture into a lined 7in (18cm) square or 8in (20cm) round tin and bake at 140°C, 275°F or Gas 1–2 for about 3½–4 hours.

Half this amount for a 13cm (5in) square or a 15cm (6in) round.
Double this amount for a 23cm (9in) square or a 25cm (10in) round.

WHISKED OR FATLESS SPONGE

90g (3oz) plain flour (sieved well and left in warm place)
3 large eggs
125g (4oz) castor sugar
few drops warm water

Whisk the sugar and eggs until the mixture is thick and creamy and a trail is left on the surface when the whisk is removed. Very gently and carefully fold the flour into the whisked eggs and sugar (never beat this in). The mixture should resemble lightly whipped cream, and if it is too thick then the eggs were probably too small, so fold in a few drops of warm water. Spoon the mixture into a prepared 20cm (8in) tin and bake in the centre of a preheated oven 180°C, 350°F or Gas 4 for approximately 30 minutes. Cool for 2–3 minutes in the tin and then turn out onto a wire rack or sugared silicone paper.

MADEIRA CAKE

185g (6oz) unsalted butter
185g (6oz) castor sugar
185g (6oz) self-raising flour
90g (3oz) plain flour
2 standard eggs
1 tsp lemon juice

Cream the butter and sugar until the mixture is light and fluffy. Beat the eggs and gradually add a little at a time to the creamed mixture, and beat until the mix is smooth and glossy. Sieve the flours thoroughly and fold into the mixture, then add lemon juice. Turn mixture into two 18cm (7in) square or 20cm (8in) round greased shallow sandwich tins and bake for 30–35 minutes at 180°C, 350°F or Gas 4 in pre-heated oven.

Also makes a chocolate cake—with the addition of 50g (2oz) cocoa powder to the flour.

QUICK ALL-IN-ONE MADEIRA CAKE

500g (1lb) plain flour
10ml (2 teaspoons) baking powder
440g (14oz) castor sugar
440g (14oz) soft margarine
7 medium eggs
50ml (3½ tablespoons) milk

Sift the flour and baking powder into a mixing bowl. Add the sugar, eggs and milk and mix together. Beat for one minute with an electric mixer or two to three minutes by hand. Put the mixture into a prepared 20cm (8in) square or 23cm (9in) round tin and bake in a preheated oven at 160°C, 325°F or Gas 3 for 1¾ to 2 hours.

CHOCOLATE CAKE RECIPE

This recipe makes a dense, moist chocolate cake which is ideal for complementing the lighter-coloured madeira in our chequerboard cake.

125g (4oz) plain chocolate
2 tablespoons coffee liqueur
125g (4oz) unsalted butter
3 large eggs (separated)
155g (5oz) castor sugar
155g (5oz) plain flour

Melt the chocolate, stirring in the butter and liqueur, and set aside. Whisk the egg whites and half of the sugar until the whites hold a peak. Beat the yolks with the rest of the sugar until the mixture is thick and ribbonlike. This is best done over a double boiler, containing warm water. Add the chocolate mixture, folding it in a little at a time. Now add the whisked egg whites and the flour, a little of each at a time. Don't overmix, just until the whole mixture is smooth.

Pour the resulting batter into a 20cm (8in) round tin and bake for 30 minutes at 160°C, 325°F or Gas 3.

ROYAL ICING RECIPE

500g (1lb) sieved icing sugar
90ml (3fl oz) water
15g (½oz) pure powdered albumen

Mix the albumen powder with the water. Leave for half an hour until the coagulated mixture has dissolved. Strain into a mixing bowl and add half the sugar, then beat in a mixer until smooth. Add to the rest of the sugar and continue beating for about 10 minutes at low speed. This icing has reached the right consistency when it has a satin-like appearance and can stand up in soft peaks.

Royal icing can also be made with natural egg white—350g (12oz) icing sugar to one egg white. Break up the egg white with a palette knife and add the icing sugar a desertspoonful at a time. Beat it thoroughly by hand between additions of sugar. A squeeze of lemon juice will help to give the icing a whiter appearance.

For royal icing to be used for covering a cake, add one teaspoon of glycerine for each 500g (1lb) of icing sugar used.

WHITE FROSTING

125g (4 oz) white vegetable fat (Trex, White Flora, Crisco)
500g (1lb) sifted icing sugar
1 teaspoon vanilla or butter essence
Pinch salt
3 tablespoons milk

Soften the fat and add the essence and salt. Beat in the sugar a quarter at a time. Scrape down the sides of the bowl often to make sure that the sugar is well mixed. Add the milk and whisk at high speed until the frosting is light and fluffy.

Keep well covered in the fridge when not in use.

To make the frosting softer for fine piping and for filling cakes, thin with an additional 2 tablespoons of milk.

The frosting can be made with half butter and half vegetable fat, but the resulting icing will be cream in colour.

INSTANT PETAL PASTE (Pastillage)

15ml (1 tablespoon) hot water
155g (5oz) Petal Paste powder
½ tsp white vegetable fat

Pour the hot water into a mixing bowl and sieve seven-eighths of the powder into the water, stirring until all the powder is incorporated. Leave the bowl covered for about five minutes. The remaining powder should be sieved onto a clean work surface, and the premixed paste kneaded thoroughly into it, until the entire mixture is smooth and elastic.

For more plasticity add ½ teaspoon white vegetable fat to the finished paste. Store in an airtight container. For best results it should be left for 24 hours. This paste must be kneaded again before use.

PASTILLAGE—GUM PASTE (1)

250g (8oz) sieved icing sugar
15ml (3 teaspoons gum tragacanth (or CMC)
5ml (1 teaspoon) liquid glucose
25–30ml (5–6 teaspoons) cold water

Sieve the icing sugar and gum tragacanth together. Make a well in the centre of the sugar and add the teaspoon of liquid glucose. Add the water and mix well. Leave to stand for 24 hours, well wrapped, in an airtight container.

PASTILLAGE—GUM PASTE (2)

500g (1lb) sifted icing sugar
1 egg white size 2 (second largest)
3 teaspoons (15ml) gum tragacanth or CMC
2 teaspoons (10ml) liquid glucose
2 teaspoons (10ml) gelatine
5 teaspoons (25ml) cold water
2 teaspoons (10ml) white fat (e.g. Trex, Cookeen, Copha)

Heat sugar and gum tragacanth in a large bowl over a saucepan of hot water. Make sure that the top of the sugar is covered, so that it doesn't get a crust.

At the same time sponge (or soak) the gelatine for about half an hour in the cold water.

Dissolve liquid glucose, white fat and gelatine over very low heat (in a second bowl of hot water is adequate).

Once the sugar is warm to the touch, start to stir the sugar on slow speed. Add the liquids (glucose mix) and the egg white. Turn machine to maximum speed and beat for about 15 minutes. The longer and harder it is beaten, the whiter it will appear.

N.B. All these pastes will dry very quickly once they are exposed to the air. If you have any difficulty in working any of them—in other words, if they are drying too quickly for you—then mix the pastillage (or gum paste) half and half with sugarpaste to get a very good modelling paste.

It will take a bit longer to dry, and will not have quite the strength of a pastillage.

GUM ARABIC SOLUTION (GLUE)

Use in the proportions of 3:1 of water to gum arabic powder, i.e. 3 teaspoons of water to 1 teaspoon of gum arabic. Measure water into a small screw-top jar and add gum arabic powder—shake well until powder has dissolved.

MODELLING CHOCOLATE

185g (6oz) chocolate—dark, milk or white
155g (5oz) liquid glucose (corn syrup)

Melt the chocolate and warm the glucose. This can either be done in the microwave—30 seconds on low—or by warming the chocolate over a bowl of hot water and standing the jar of glucose in hot water. Stir the glucose into the melted chocolate, mix well and knead into a paste. Wrap it in silicone paper and leave it overnight.

GANACHE—lovely for the inside of a chocolate sponge!

This is a chocolate filling made of cream, chocolate and flavouring.

125g (4oz) cream
185g (6oz) of dark chocolate or 220g (7oz) milk or white chocolate

Bring the cream to the boil. Remove from heat and add the finely chopped chocolate and stir until it is smooth. Leave until cool. For piping or coating, the ganache can be whisked until it is light and fluffy.

CUTTING CAKES

The plans shown below suggest the most practical procedures for cutting tiered cakes. Only the square and round ones are easy to cut without a certain amount of waste. An oval shape is the most inefficient in this respect, as unless there are guests with a particular liking for icing, several of the portions taken from the sides will be unusable.

The number of portions yielded depends on whether the cakes are made from a fruit cake or a sponge-based recipe. In general, a slice taken from a sponge wedding cake is twice the size of that from a fruit cake.

The cutting plan for the examples shown in the diagram, which are all for three-tier cakes, are as follows:

SPONGE CAKES

Round	Small	15cm (6in)	16
	Medium	25cm (10in)	48
	Large	36cm (14in)	96
Square	Small	15cm (6in)	18
	Medium	25cm (10in)	68
	Large	36cm (14in)	98
Hexagon	Small	15cm (6in)	6
	Medium	25cm (10in)	18
	Large	36cm (14in)	52

FRUIT CAKES

Round	Small	15cm (6in)	20
	Medium	25cm (10in)	35
	Large	36cm (14in)	140
Square	Small	15cm (6in)	25
	Medium	25cm (10in)	70
	Large	36cm (14in)	160

Hexagon, Oval, Heart and Petal all cut to approximately the same size

	Small	15cm (6in)	30
	Medium	20cm (8in)	50
	Large	30cm (12in)	85
	Extra Large	36cm (14in)	120

PRESERVING CAKES AND MODELS

It is possible to freeze most cakes for several months, but this is only recommended if they have not been decorated. Once they are iced, the condensation which is formed on their surface as they defrost causes the decoration to run, and the icing to get very sticky. It is far better to keep a decorated sponge cake for no longer than a few days, a week at the most. A rich fruit cale, if properly iced, should keep for up to a year, as the marzipan and icing layers seal the cake from the air around it and stop it drying out or going rancid. All decorated cakes are best stored in plain cardboard cake boxes away from too much heat or humidity.

Marzipan, chocolate and pastillage models benefit from a light coating of edible confectioner's glaze if you wish to preserve them, although in the case of marzipan figures, this only extends their life by about two weeks. In order to keep them indefinitely, two or three layers of glaze may be applied, but this causes them to become inedible.

A spray of pastillage flowers from the top of a cake can be preserved for years if it is protected from humidity and strong light. Ideally it should be wired to a pad of fabric or a piece of cork, and placed in a small display case so that it can be seen and enjoyed. Silica gel helps to keep the flowers dry. Put a few crystals in the case, with the spray, and if they change colour from blue to pink they should be removed, dried in a warm oven and then replaced.

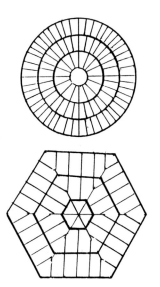
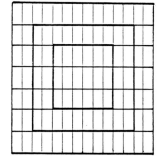

Cutting chart for sponge cakes

PILLARS AND TEMPLATES

The layers of a tiered wedding cake have to be supported, and the usual practice is to use plastic or plaster pillars. On a sugarpaste, fondant or frosted cake, the pillars are only for decoration as all the weight of the cake above is supported by skewers which pass right through the cake to its cake board. Each supporting tier has its own set of skewers and pillars.

In order to position the skewers and pillars correctly, a set of templates cut in thin card should be made for each shape of tin.

Square tins

Make a 20cm (8in) and a 25cm (10in) square in thin card. Draw a diagonal line from corner to corner and measure out from the centre point in 1cm (½in) increments. At the 6cm (2½in) mark (from the centre) draw a small circle around the point, at the 7cm (3in) mark draw a square, and at the 8cm (3½in) mark draw a diamond.

The circle (or 6cm mark) is for the 20cm (8in) cake
The square (or 7cm mark) is for the 25cm (10in) cake
The diamond (or 8cm mark) is for the 30cm (12in) cake

Round tins

Make a 20cm (8in) and a 25cm (10in) circle in thin card. Fold in half then into half again—so that the template is divided into four. Mark out the measurements from the centre point using the same method as for the square.

It is important to ensure that each tier sits flat and level. When checking the cake, be sure that it too is sitting on a perfectly horizontal surface!

The first step is to use the template to find the right position for the pillars. Rest the pillars on the cake and place a ruler across their tops. Use a spirit level to check that the surface of the cakes is horizontal by measuring along the top of the ruler.

If everything is perfect, slide the ruler along the tops of the pillars and extend it past the edge of the cake. Hold the first of the skewers vertically with its point resting on the cake board, and its side just touching the ruler. Mark it at this position, then cut the top part off. What remains is a skewer which is the combined height of the cake, the pillar, and the thickness of the ruler. Cut the others to the same length, and push them into the cake. When the pillars are placed over them, the end of the skewer should protrude about 3.5mm (⅛in). This means that when a cake is placed above them, its weight is borne by the skewer, not the pillar.

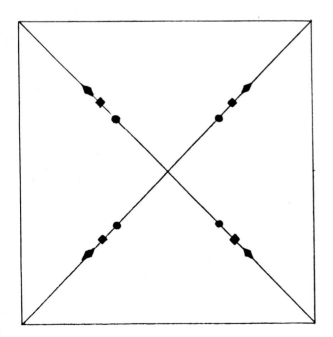

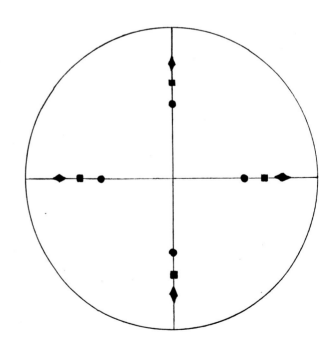